THE PRESS IN INDIA

THE PRESS IN INDIA

PARTHA SARKAR

Akansha Publishing House
• Delhi • Guwahati • Visakhapatnam

AKANSHA PUBLISHING HOUSE
4649-B/21, Ansari Road
Daryaganj, New Delhi-110002
Phones: 23268193, 09435116718
Email: ektabooks@yahoo.com
visit us: www.akanshapublishinghouse.com

The Press in India

First Published 2012

ISBN 978-81-8370-317-8

PRINTED IN INDIA

Published by Akansha Publishing House, New Delhi-110002 and printed at Harmain Offset Printers, Delhi.

To

My Parents

Foreword

The book, *The Press in India*, by Dr. Partha Sarkar, Assistant Professor in the Department of Mass Communication, Assam University, Silchar is a useful addition to the literature on the Indian Press, specifically the press in the Barak Valley of Southern Assam. It is a brave attempt to present a matter-of-fact picture of the press in the valley, it trials and tribulations, the contribution for the uplift of the society and also its future.

The historical perspective provides a window to the past, of both the Indian Press and journalism in Assam. Then narrows its focus to the press in the valley during the British colonial period. The subsequent evaluation of the Post-Independence period is noteworthy. The contemporary trends, both technological and economic, could have been more exploratory and analytical. Today, as all of us know, media are technology-driven and the press in Barak Valley has also come under its impact.

The unique geographical location of Barak Valley is responsible for the different types of content in the regional press. Ethnic and cultural diversities coupled with multiplicity of languages have their own influence on the press. The creeping of tabloidisation in the mainstream print media at the national level is a matter of serious concern and the press in Barak Valley is also slowly getting impacted by the trend.

The media, particularly, is the watchdog of any democratic system and the Indian press has done an admirable service to the polity. A clear and exhaustive analysis of the role of the regions press could have added more colour to the work. I expect many more meaningful and relevant publications from Dr. Partha Sarkar, Which in turn should be thought-provoking for both academics and professionals. I wish him every success in all his scholarly endeavours.

Prof. K.V. Nagraj
Deptt. of Mass Communication
Assam University
Silchar, Assam

Preface

The book “The Press in India” is aimed to analytically explore the historical evolution of the press in Barak Valley in terms of its origin, growth and development, i.e., emergence, expansion and qualitative formations over a period of over two centuries. The status, contributing factors and historical patterns of the press in Barak Valley are the specific objects which have been investigated and analytically presented in this book.

During the British rule in India, the then Surma Valley played an important role in the history of journalism. Since the partition of India in 1947 the Barak Valley journalism has been discharging her obligation to the nation for social upliftment. .As part of the history of vernacular press in India the press of this valley has contributed so many dailies and periodicals. But no significant effort has so far been made to reveal the nature of journalism in the Barak Valley. So, the objective of the study is to know about the nature of Barak Valley journalism-its origin, growth and development .On what ground the press stands in this remotest valley of India is also a considerable point of the study. On celebration of the 150 years of Assam Journalism one gets a special opportunity to have a glimpse of the glorious role played by the press in Barak Valley.

As required by its nature, objectives and design, the study is based on documentary, historical, oral and official data. The historical experiences and documents preserved with personalities and official establishments of press or otherwise form the crux of the information used in the book. The sources providing data on the press in Barak Valley have been tapped comprehensively to analyse the contribution of the regional press in the nation-building process in India as well as in reflecting and influencing historical evolution of the society in Barak Valley itself. The book is organized into ten chapters, in all.

Partha Sarkar

Acknowledgements

The journey of thousand miles begins with a single step. The journey, in fact, started on April 19th 2003, when came in the Department of Mass Communication, Assam University, Silchar. This journey was encouraged, supported and cooperated by my Prof . G.P. Pandey, Dean, School of Information Science , without whose guidance this book would not have seen the light of the day. At first, I express my gratitude to him for the evergreen support I have received. My special thanks are to Prof. K V Nagaraj, Department of Mass Communication, Assam University, Silchar., who has been very kind to me to extend any kind of help during the work. I would like to acknowledge the advice and moral support in this work extended to me by Prof. G. Ram, Department of Sociology. I am highly grateful to Mr. Jyotilal Choudhury for his valuable suggestions, encouragement and support.

Professor Subhash Chandra Saha, ex-Vice Chancellor, Assam University, Silchar, is a dynamic force behind the multifarious development of this maturing university. He is a dynamic, generous and sensitive personality, who is always ready to support and encourage the students and scholars academically and morally. Through my journalistic activities I, too, received his attention. His queries, advice, encouragement and moral support during the work provided me a great strength and inspiration. I am highly thankful to him for such kind of his benign gestures.

I take this opportunity to thank Prof. Gopalji Mishra, Department of Social Work and Prof Subir Kar, Retd Prof, Department of Bengali, Assam University, Silchar for their constant inspiration.

My debt is due to Mr. Santanu Ghosh, Editor Jogashankha, Dr. M. Sham, Mr. Mridul Roy, Mr. Samarjit Choudhury, Mr. H. R. Choudhury, Mr. Arijit Adirya and Mr. Partha Bhattacharya, who very graciously extend their cooperation without which the whole exercise would have been inconceivable. I am thankful to all of them.

My heartfelt thanks are to my friends - Maitrayan, Kalapi, Chumki, Pankaj, Dibakar, Pritiwish and Arindam, the then faculty of the Lakhotia Computer Centre, Silchar- who supported and inspired me.

My Dadu an inspirator, supporter and encourager Mr. Ardhandu Bhattacharya, always stands with me. His son Arnav, also helped me in composing of the book on my computer. Both deserve thanks-a lot

I would like to thank my students who cooperated and extended help whenever needed for completion of this study.

While preparing this book I took note of valuable suggestions from friends and colleagues in the profession. I would like to acknowledge the assistance and advice received from them at different stages of the research work.

Last but not the least, I acknowledge my family members, my parents, my wife and my son Gairik, who helped and supported me during the period.

Partha Sarkar

Contents

1

Execution of the Study

The Problem

The desire to communicate, to exchange ideas, to learn about the changes in the immediate environment and to seek the truth is inherent in human nature. Communication of news and views is an integral part of human life. Man is always eager to know what is going around him and what people are thinking about various events and developments. He has used different means in different times to fulfill this need.

In ancient times, before the advent of newspaper, radio and television, news was communicated by words of mouth. Public announcements by those who are in power were communicated to the people by drummers. With the invention of printing press, the process becomes easier. Setting up of printing press led to publication of bulletins, newspapers, books, and magazines in different parts of the world. The purpose was to serve the people by reporting and interpreting what is happening in the world around them.

From its fundamental importance for social development, communication has in all societies a development policy and point of view. Communication as a means of transmission of information and as a process of development has gone under many changes with the invention of printing press. It was however strengthened and stabilized with publication of newspapers. Over the years the press has been playing a dominant role in dissemination of news and information.

As a magnificent gift to mankind and highly indispensable, the press performs its crucial role as communicator. It is a major force and is forming public opinion the world over. It effects national and global efforts towards socio-economic progress and understanding. It touches almost every aspect of our public life. Because of its importance and significance it has been highly acclaimed, admired and appreciated. A society needs newspaper for the same reason as a man needs eyes. It has to see where it is going to It would not be unacceptable to say that air is to the living beings; the press is to the society. The study makes an attempt to discuss comprehensively the origin, growth and development of the press with special reference to Barak valley of Assam.

Survey of Literature

The press is powerful and effective political communicator in India and has encountered challenges from various quarters. A significant number of studies have been made on it. Rau Chalapathi (1968) in his study of the press in India covered various aspects of press - its pattern, internal freedom, relationship between the editor and proprietor, etc. Mankekar (1973), in his book 'The Press under Pressure', has expressed his deep concern for the impatience and intolerance showed by the Indian rulers towards the press. He deplored that the press has been under the control of authorities through subtle means. He described the ordeals that the press underwent during the national emergency in 1975. Kuldip Nayar (1977) vividly described how the press in India was harassed and its freedom was muzzled during the national emergency. Srivastava (1972), in his study of 'Media Issues', made an attempt to discuss how the media, particularly print media have been threatened by militants. His work covered a wide variety of subjects. Padhy (1991), in his book 'Battle for Freedom of Press in India', discussed how the press has been humbled by authorities including the executive, legislative, judiciary, terrorists and the management of press itself. Krishna Murthy Nadig (1966), in his work 'Indian Journalism', made sincere study of the growth, development and role of the press in India since the early days of James Augustus Hicky. Parthasarathy Rangaswamy (1989), in his study 'Journalism in India', did the best to write a historically meaningful story of Indian journalism from the days of Hicky to modern times. Raghavan (1994) in his study 'Press in India' provided a comprehensive description of Indian press since the time of Hicky's Gazette. Bhatta (1997) in his study of 'Indian Press since 1955' provided a description of all the latest developments that have taken place since 1955.

In his book 'Contemporary Issues in Journalism' (1988) Rahul Mudgal has discussed various manifestations of what might be called the new journalism and its influence on the main stream or traditional journalism to highlight the information revolution and knowledge explosion. The role of press and journalism has become very crucial, though the practice of journalism varies from country to country.

In the book 'Press - Inside Outside' Rama Vajpayee's (2002) main thrust is to highlight the role of press, media and television which have deep links with numerous of socio-economic and commercial programmes of our society. Besides, the book has covered several significant aspects like the press, its freedom, role of television, its growth and changing role of the news media and various types of advertisement. The contents deal with new ideas and trends.

Swati Chauhan and Navin Chandra (1997) in their book 'Journalism Today - Principle Practices and Challenges', described the importance of the journalist's work and its importance. Like any other professional with a high degree of knowledge, skill and perception, a true journalist is also constantly striving for professional excellence. Apart from the topics dealt with such as news, values, etc. there is an emphasis on the application of news printing technology and development perspective in the contemporary press.

'Press in Assam : Origin and Development' (1999) by Sunil Pawan Baruah reveals the first one hundred years' history of the journalism in Assam in a wider perspective of the Indian press. The book makes a chronological survey of the press in the region dealing with original material and documents. Each chapter throws interesting light of the publication on newspapers, journals and periodicals of the time and takes an account of the contemporary socio-political and economic conditions of the North-Eastern region.

'*Srihatta-Sahitaya Parisat O Patrik*a' (1996) by Dr. Usharanjan Bhattachajee dealt with newspapers and magazines published from Sylheth (Bangladesh). The book is divided into two parts. The first part deals with the organization of newspapers and the second part deals with gradual growth of the newspapers for the last two centuries.

Jatindra Mohan Bhattacharjee (1943) in his book '*Shree Hattabasi Sanpadita Abong Shreehatta O Cachar Haite Prakasito Sanbadpatra*' presents a clear picture of newspapers and periodicals published from Shree Hatta (now in Bangladesh) and Cachar which is present Barak Valley. Further, this book deals with the illustration of the newspapers and concerned journalist.

Mahi Uddin Siru (1992) in his book "Sylhter Satabarser Sangbatikata" gives a lucid picture of the newspapers and periodicals which were published from Sylhet district. It is helpful in enlisting the press publication of the pre-Independence era.

Satabdir Tathya Punji (1998) compiled and edited by a cultural organization, *Barak Upataka Banga Sahitya Samileyan* consists of various articles written by veteran journalists of Barak Valley. In this volume one finds the listing of various newspapers in the Barak Valley. Further, one of the articles deals with language movement which is highlighted properly.

It appears that the literature on the press has been mostly enriched by the professionals who have drawn from their own vast experience in the field of journalism. The literature has been shaped by their own feelings, impressions, attitudes and values. On many issues, they have remained one-sided with their professionalism by ignoring the reality of socio-political problems and facts. On the other hand, the legal practitioners who have dealt with the various aspects of the press in their work are more legalistic in their approach. They have not discussed in detail about the origin, growth and development of the press in the socio-political context of India. Finally, there are many studies, particularly on the press in Assam and Barak Valley which provide a systematic or chronological account of the press publications in a general manner. All of these have not been able to discuss the press by relating it with society, state and history in a given context. Therefore, the existing literature suffers from certain deficiencies. The present study has tried to provide a systematic and comprehensive analysis of the origin, growth and development of Indian press with special reference to Barak Valley of Assam.

In the Barak Valley the first newspaper was published more than a century after the publication of the‘ Bengal Gazette ’. The first newspaper of Barak valley ‘Silchar’ was published in Bengali, which appeared in 1886 from Silchar. Since then the era of journalism began in the valley. In the context a question springs up.

What is the nature of origin, growth and development of the press observed during its historical evolution in the North Eastern region in India, specially in the Barak Valley of Assam state?

Key Terms

The study has used the following key terms along with their meanings:

Development: ‘Development’ refers to the qualitative transformations of the press in the Barak Valley.

Growth: ‘Growth’ refers to the expansion in size of the press in the Barak Valley.

Origin: 'Origin' refers to the conditions and nature of emergence of the press in the Barak Valley.

Press: In modern context, the term press is primarily applied to daily, bi-weekly or weekly newspaper, magazines, and periodicals In the present study this meaning of the term is followed.

Objectives

The aim of the study is to reveal the origin, growth, and development of the press in Barak Valley of Assam. The specific objectives of the study are as follows:

i) To examine the status of press in the Barak Valley by enlisting the different types of newspapers and periodicals which have been or are being published from the Barak Valley

ii) To examine the contributions of different persons or journalists to the growth of press in the valley

iii) To find out the factors that led to the birth of newspapers in the valley

iv) To understand the patterns of origin, growth and development of the press in the valley

v) To understand the impact of press on socio-economic development of the valley

Hypothesis

The study is designed for descriptive research of the historical evolution of the press in Barak Valley. No hypothesis is therefore formulated here. The findings of this study are supposed to generate new problems and hypotheses for the studies on press as to be conducted in future.

Data and Methodology

The study is basically descriptive in nature and utilizes the historical and empirical data about the press in the Barak

Valley. The data reveal the socio-political conditions and mechanisms (processes) of origin, growth and development of the press. The historical journey of the press along with its twists and terns is depicted through a systematic account of events, personalities and their consequences.

Sources of Data and Method of Analysis

This study dealing with the origin, growth and development of press in Barak Valley is mainly historical research based. The earlier works in this field have been used by applying document analysis method. The data, facts and figures have been obtained from the available books, journals and official records. The eminent personalities, experienced persons, experts, performers have been interviewed in order to get an insight and detailed picture. 50 eminent personalities and journalist were interviewed from Cachar, Karimganj and Hailakandi district to assess the impact of press in the Barak Valley. The area of the study is Barak Valley.

Area of the Study

The study has been conducted in Barak Valley of Assam. The Barak valley which derives its name from the river 'Barak' situated in the southern part of Assam consists of three districts; namely, Cachar, Karimganj and Hailakandi, covering an area of 6922 sq km. The valley is bounded by Bangladesh in the west, Meghalaya in the north, Manipur in the east, and Mizoram and Tripura in the south. Its current population is 24,91,546 (Census 1991).

The Barak Valley is the natural extension of the adjoining Bengal plains. Social formation through the ages was on the same line as in Bengal. In spite of the Manipuri settlement since Burmese occupation of Manipur in 1818 AD and the immigration of the north Indian labours since the introduction of tea plantation in 1855 AD by the Britishers, more than 80 % of the people in Barak Valley today are Bengalis. According to the Census Report 1971, nearly 80 % of the total population was Bengali. At that time total population was 1743400. Of these 1332200 were Bengali. Hindi speaking people were 1,01,500; Manipuri were 101500, Dimasa were 9200 and the rest 6800 were Ahomia, Naga, Mizo, etc. (Statistical Handbook, Assam, 1992).

The Barak Valley is now full fledged region having all the avenues for further prosperity. Facilities for education from primary to university level are available here. Central University, National Institute of Technology, Medical College, Research Centre, Agricultural Training Institute, etc. serve the needs of this region in different spheres. Moreover, one airport is also there to connect this remote region with the rest of the country. The 'Cachar Paper Mill' located at Panchgram of this valley is the biggest paper mill in Asia. Radio and TV Centres are also functioning here since long time. Silchar which is the headquarter of Cachar district is a developed city in the Barak Valley. The valley is rich in resources and one of the country's most thickly populated areas.

Organisation of the Study

The study tentatively consists of ten chapters as given below.

Chapter 1: *Execution of the Study*: This chapter comprises the problem of research and its scope, survey of literature, objectives and methodology for the study

Chapter 2: *The Barak Valley*: This chapter discusses the geographical, historical, demographic, social, cultural, economic and political features of Barak Valley in Assam.

Chapter 3: *Press in the Historical Perspective:* This chapter deals with the historical perspective of Indian press in terms of its evolution.

Chapter 4: *The Indian Press:* This chapter brings out the patterns of historical emergence, expansion and qualitative unfoldings of the Indian press to understand a linkage of the press in Barak Valley with the wider Indian context.

Chapter 5: *The Press in Assam:* This chapter discusses the Assamese Journalism in its pre and post -Independence period.

Chapter 6: *The Barak Valley Press in the British Period*: This chapter analyses the origin, growth and development of the press during the British period in terms of its status, contributing factors and emerging patterns

Chapter 7: *The Barak Valley Press in the Post-Independence Period*: This chapter delineates the status, contributing factors and patterns of the press during the Post-Independence period.

Chapter 8: *The Barak Valley Press in the Contemporary Time*: This chapter gives an account of the status, factor and trends of the press in the contemporary times.

Chapter 9: *Socio-economic Impact of the Barak Valley Press*: This chapter analyses the role and impact of press on the socio-economic development of Barak Valley

Chapter 10: *Summary, Findings and Conclusion*: This Chapter makes a summary of the study and derives some major findings and conclusions.

Scope of the Study

The study deals with the origin, growth and development of journalism in Barak valley. The journalism in Barak valley had been growing since the colonial era but there has been no serious effort to analyse the press in Barak Valley. There is a greater need to systematically study the background of journalism in Barak valley. The 150 years of celebration of journalism in Assam provided special opportunity to study the glorious role played by the press since its inception in Barak Valley.

REFERENCES

Barketaki, S 1969 *Assam, New* Delhi: National Book Trust.

Bashiruddin, S 1980 *Rural Press in India, AMIC*: Bangalore.

Dutta, P.N. 1962 *Glimpses into the History of Assam,* Guwahati.

Ghosh, Subir 1991 *Mass Media Today,* Calcutta: Profile Publisher.

Government of Assam 1971 *Census Report of Assam,* Directorate Census Operator, Assam.

Government of Assam 1991 *Census Report of Assam,* Directorate Census Operator, Assam.

Government of Assam 2001 *Census Report of Assam,* Directorate Census Operator, Assam.

Government of Assam 2003 *Statistical Handbook of Assam* Directorate of Economics and Statistics, Guwahati : Government of Assam.

Government of Assam 2004 *Statistical Handbook of Assam* Directorate of Economics and Statistics, Guwahati : Government of Assam.

Mudgal Rahul 1998 *Contemporary Issues in Journalism,* New Delhi: Sarup & Sons.

Mulgaokar, M.S 1984 *The Press in India,* Bombay: Popular Prakashan.

Nath, R.M. 1981 *Antiquities of Cachar*, Silchar.

Rau Chalapathi, M 1980 "200 Years of Indian Press", *Vidura:* February.

2

The Barak Valley

The Barak Valley is a region with its distinct geography, history, culture and society in the state of Assam in India. Such a distinction makes a difference to the press and patterns of communication. Therefore, the valley needs to be introduced as the area of the present study.

Physiography

The three districts of southern Assam - Cachar, Hailakandi and Karimganj-together constitute Barak Valley, which in the pre-Independence period was a part of the erstwhile Surma Valley. The valley is situated between longitudes 92° 15' and 93° 15' and latitudes 24° 8' and 25° 8'. It is bounded on the north by the North Cachar Hills of Assam and Jaintia Hills district of Megalaya; on the east by Manipur; on the south by Mizoram and on the west by Tripura and Sylhet district of Bangladesh. The total area of Barak Valley is 6,922 sq. kms, of which Cachar district alone accounts for 57. 4% of the total area; the shares of Hailakandi and Karimganj district being 19. 2% and 26. 1% respectively. The total population of Barak Valley as per the census Report (2001) census was 29,88,797 lakhs with a literacy rate of 56. 6%. Until recently the Barak Valley area was 'Cachar' district in its unified form. In fact, since 1983 when Karimganj sub-division was declared a district, the areas of the old Cachar district (of post-Independence period) came to be known as ' Barak Valley' as a mark of distinction from the Assam Valley proper. At present, the old Cachar district (of post-Independence period) stands trifurcated as Hailakandi sub-division was also declared a district in 1989. It is to be noted here that after Independence, Cachar district had four sub-divisions – Hailakandi, Karimganj, North Cachar Hills and Silchar. But in 1952, North Cachar Hills was separated from Cachar and since then Cachar District meant present Barak Valley area till 1983. In fact, Cachar district of the period (1951-1983) is today's Barak Valley (Ahmed 1998). The area of the present valley and its constituent districts is shown in the following table.

Table 2.1: Area of the Barak Valley

(in Sq km)

District	Area
Cachar	3786
Karimganj	1809
Hailakandi	1327
Total	6922

Source: Government of Assam 2004, *Statistical Handbook of Assam*, Directorate of Economics and Statistics, Assam Topography.

The topography of the valley is composed of high hills, low lands and level plains. Vast tracts in the southern part of the valley are covered with forests. The valley is almost shut in by the hill ranges on the north, east and south which occupy considerable area of the valley's territory. Nearly the whole of the valley is dotted with scattered low- range hills which are locally called 'tillahs'. The river 'Barak' flows through the plains of the valley. High lands of the valley are pre-dominantly planted with tea bushes while lower portions mostly are covered by rice. In fact, tea and rice together constitute 90 percent of the valley's cropped area. Populations constitute the bulk. Around 70 percent of the working population is engaged in agriculture and other primary sector activities, which shows symptoms of a subsistence and peripheral economy. Minerals and water resources of the Barak Valley have dawn attention of many Government agencies. But the resources are yet to be explored as they require a vast investment of capital before being commercially viable (Mazumdar 1996).

Climate

The climate of the Barak Valley is favourable for cultivation of variety of crops, of which rice is the most important. Before the Green Revolution, the average yield of rice per hectare of the valley was much above the country's overall average per hectare but by 1970s the same began to fall and present average yield of the valley per hectare has fallen much below the country's average yield level and, as a result, the valley has become a rice-deficit zone. Another important surplus generating sector in Barak Valley's economy is the tea industry. Tea covers about 13.5 percent of the total cropped area and contributes significantly to the valley's Net Domestic Product. Tea is regarded as the most important surplus income generating sector in Barak Valley's economy. However, the average yield of tea per hectare in the valley is far below the state's or country's average yield per hectare.

Forest

Forests cover more than one-third of the valley's total land area. However, mass scale deforestation in recent years is resulting in the decline of forest products. Besides the forests, substantial portion of the valley's total area is occupied by barren tracts. The percentage of cultivable land in the total land is considerably low as compared to all India level. The inadequacy of cultivable land in view of a rising population has resulted to the heavier pressure on available agricultural lands and disguised unemployment in rural areas of the valley. The density of population of Barak Valley is greater than five states in North- East India of which rural (Allen 1990).

River

The Barak, the most important river of the valley. The river rises on the escarpment of the Borail ranges from the south of Jupvo Peak to the north of Manipur. Its upper part is marked by steep banks and several falls. It turns west in the Cachar district through which it flows down to a place called Haritikar near Badarpur, where it separates into two branches to rejoin at Habiganj in Bangladesh. The northern branch is called the Surma and the southern branch is called Kushiyara. The total length of the river is 560 miles before it joins the Brahmaputra. The river has numerous tributaries. The principal tributaries of the river in the Barak Valley are the Jiri, the Chiri, the Madhura, the Ghagra, the Sonai, the Jatinga, the Dhaleswari, the Katakha, the Longai and the Singal.

The Barak Valley suffers from frequent bouts of floods. Floods inflicted the valley with heavy in 1929, 1932, 1935, 1941, 1946, 1952, 1953, 1959, 1962, 1966, 1972, 1976, 1985, 1986, 1989, 1991 and 2004. The embankments constructed by the Flood Controls Department have failed to rid the valley of the flood menace (Choudhury 1992).

Soil

The general feature of the valley's soil is acidity. Some parts of the valley are capped by red loamy soil. There are the parts which are covered by lateritic soil. The Barak Valley has also numerous lakes and marshes rich in the soil with organic matters.

Flora

The valley's natural vegetation consists of the forests with the large evergreen trees forming a higher canopy and the smaller shrubs and herbs forming lower storey. Large climbers are also present in considerable numbers. The important species are Garjun (*Dipterocarpus turbinatus*), Nahor (*Mcsua fkerrea*), Kurta (*Palaquium polyanthum*), Nagalichi (*Nephelium longana*), Kendu (*Diospyros toposia*), Marhal (*Vetica *lanceafolia*), Jinari (*Podocarpus nerifolium*), Jaman (*Eugenia* sp.), Dhuna (*Canarium* sp.), Chickrassi (*Chikrassia tabularies*), Sundri, Cham (*Artocarpus chaplasa*). The species Jinari, which occurs only in the Cachar region and Eastern Assam, is of great botanical interest as it is one of the few conifers having broad leaves. Different species of bamboos are also found in the valley. They are chiefly Muli (Melocanna bambusoides), Pecha (*Dendro calemus* Hamiltonil), Dolu (*Leinostachyum dullua*) Makal (*B. palida*) (Barkakati 1989).

Fauna

(i) Wild life depends directly or indirectly on vegetation for food and habitat. The extensive forests of the valley were the home of different kinds of wild animals like tigers, leopards, bears, elephants, wild dogs, deers, porcupines and foxes. There were also different kinds of reptiles and birds. The valley, which was rich in different forms of wild life, even in the early post-Independence period, has lost most of these because of deforestation and hunting. The only wild animals, often come across here, are wild elephants.

(ii) Domestic animals of the valley are cows, buffaloes, pigs, goats, sheep, and dogs. The domestic birds are fowls, ducks and pigeons etc (Barkakati 1989).

Population

Linguistically, the Bengali speaking people form the majority of the valley's population. Besides the Bengalis, there are also other communities inhabiting the valley. They are chiefly the Manipuris, the Kukis, the Nagas, the Khasis, the Barmans, the Triparas, the Assamese, the Hmars and the Nepalese. There are also the people brought in the valley as the workers in the tea gardens in the valley. They came from different parts of the country like Bengal, Bihar, Eastern U. P. and Orissa. They belong to different caste groups like Santhal, the Hoe, the Mundas and the Orans. According to the census Report (1991), the total population of the valley was, 24, 91,496 (Goswami 1991) and while in 2001 it is 29,88,797. The population distribution of the today's valley is shown in Table 2.2.

Table 2.2: Total Population of Barak Valley

District	Population	%
Cachar	14,4,141	48
Karimganj	10,03,678	34
Hailakandi	5,42,978	18
Total	29,88,797	100

Source: Census Report of India, Assam State 2001, Directorate of Census Operation, Assam.

Table 2.2 shows that Cachar distict has almost half of the valley's population, whereas Karimganj has over a one third and Hailakandi has about a one fifth of the population.

Distribution of population on the rural-urbal basis and its patterns have impacts on the development of a press. Therefore, rural-urban distribution of the valley's population is given in Table 2.3.

Table 2.3: Rural and Urban Population

District	Rural	%	Urban	%
Cachar	12,40,723	46.4	2,01418	62.8
Karimganj	93,0131	35	73,547	23
Hailakandi	49,7421	18.6	45,557	14.2
Total	2,66,8275	100	3,20,522	100

Source: Census Report of India, Assam State 2001, Directorate of Census Operation, Assam.

Table 2.3 shows that in the valley the Cachar district harbours about half of the rural population and over three fifths of the urban population followed by Karimganj district with over a one third and about one fourth population respectively.

Density of Population

The density of the population in the valley is shown in Table 2.4

Table 2.4: Density of the population in per sq. km in the Barak Valley

(Persons per square kilometres)

2001	1991	1971	1961	1951	1941	1931	1921
449	372	246	197	160	128	115	107

Source: *Statistical Handbook of Assam*2004, Directorate of Economics and Statistics, Assam.

The figures reveal that the density of the population of Barak Valley is higher than the density of population in Assam as a whole. The rate of increase in density of population in the valley is also higher than that in the state of Assam. While in Assam, the density of population rose from 186 in 1971 to 284 in 1991, the density in the Barak Valley increased from 246 per sq. km. in 1971 to 372 in 1991 and to 449 in 2001

The Barak Valley is, therefore, densely populated in comparison with the state as a whole. The higher rate of increase of population is due to several factors. In the North East the valley was comparatively free from the political turmoil during the recent decades. Only some low intensity insurgency-related troubles showed their teeth in the fringe areas of the valley.

Population Growth

The Barak Valley witnesses the migration of easy flow, though it may not be torrents. People come also in some. It is now necessary to take a look at the growth of population in the valleyThe following table shows the decadal percentage variations in populations since 1901 in the three districts of Barak Valley.

Table 2.5: Population variation in the Barak valley District

Year	Karimjanj	Hailakandi	Cachar
1901-11	12.94	16.09	12.33
1911-21	3.19	7.59	5.98
1921-31	5.91	7.08	7.60
1931-41	9.52	10.29	13.08
1941-51	29.87	17.48	23.92
1951-61	22.96	27.23	22.60
1961-71	25.13	23.61	23.96
1971-91	42.08	45.94	47.59
1991-2001	21.87	20.89	18.89

Source: Govt of Assam 2004 *Statistical Handbook of Assam*, Guwahati Directorate of Economics and Statistics, Assam.

The figures indicate that the decadal growth has registered a little more than 100 percent rise after the 1931-41 decade. The Independence and partition of the country came about towards the end of the first half of the year 1947. The continuous large-scale influx of people from East Pakistan (now Bangladesh) was undoubtedly responsible for the increase in the growth rate of population. Since then the valley's decadal growth rate of population has always been above 20 percent. The figures in the last but one period (1971-91) show the growth rate for a period of two decades 1971-81 and 1981-91 as the census operations in 1981 were not undertaken in the state due to insurgency problem. It is also found that the growth rate in the State is lower by 9.5% than the growth rate in the 20-years period 1941-61 (Goswami 1991).

Influx of people migrating from the state of Bangladesh is also leading to change in the demographic picture and ratio also. The percentage of people belonging to the Barman community has been falling since Independence, following the partition and communal disturbances in East Pakistan.

According to the Census Reports (2001), the total number of population in the valley is 29,95,769, the total population of India is 1027 million in 2001. These figures show a national decadal growth rate of 21. 35 percent for the period 1991-2001.

On the basis of the linguistic distribution of population in the Census Report (1971) the populations and percentages, of ethno-linguistic groups in the total population of the valley are given in Table 2.6.

Table 2.6: Valley's Estimated Linguistic Distribution of the population into community In the Barak Valley

Linguistic Community	Population	Percentage of the Total Population
Meithei	126984	4.2
Bishnupriya	58956	1.95
Dimasa(Barmans)	18141	0.06
Hindustani	338625	11.2
Bengalee	2343158	77.5
Others	1502566	4.55

Source: Govt of Assam 2004 *Statistical Handbook of Assam*, Guwahati, Directorate of Economics and Statistics, Assam.

The table shows that the Benganlis constitute over three fourths of the valley's population; the Hindusthani constitute over a one tenth and the rest each constitutes less than 5% of its population.

Religionwise Distribution of Population

The Hindus form a major religious community of the valley. The second largest religious community is the Muslim. There are also the Buddhists, the Christians, the Jains and a very small number of people still following the animistic tribal faiths. The animists mostly were converted to Christianity and as a result of greater in-roads made by the Christianity among the tribals, the original animistic tribals' faiths have almost become extinct. It appears from the presence of ancient shrines, temples, mosques and churches in different places of the region that the people are religious minded. Religionwise size of the communities in the population of the Barak Valley is given in Table 2.7.

Table 2.7: Population by Religion in the Barak Valley 2001

Religious Community	Population	Percentage of total population
Hindus	15,80,660	55.5
Muslims	83,4900	43.02
Christian	36,730	1.35
Jains	1,970	0.07
Sikhs	765	0.009
Buddhist	1,677	0.46
Unstated	225	0.009
Other Religion	857	0.04

Source: Government of India 2001 Census Report of Assam, Directorate of Census Operation, Assam.

The table shows that the Hindus constitute over a half of the population; where as Muslims constitute a slightly more than two thirds of the population and the rest are the communuties constituting around or less than 1% of the population in thre valley.

Table 2.8 shows that in the Barak Valley the Bengali population constitutes around two thirds of the total population in all the three districts; the Hindi speaking population constitute 7% to 9%; the Assamese constitute about 30% in Karimjanj and mominal ratio in the other two districts and Manipuries constituted a proportion between less than 1% to 6% in the three districts.

Table 2.8: Districtwise Distribution of the Linguistic Populations in the Barak Valley 2001

(in per cent)

District	Population by Language			
	Assamese	Bengali	Hindi	Manipuri
Cachar	5821 (0.41%)	918853 (63.7%)	135367 (9.3%)	84073 (5.89%)
Karimjanj	2751 (29.6%)	701513 (69.8%)	72673 (7.25%)	5005 (0.49%)
Hailakandi	698 (0.12%)	369896 (68.12%)	48005 (8.84%)	11557 (2.1%)
Total	9270 (100%)	1990262 (100%)	256045 (100%)	100635 (100%)

Source: Govt.of India 2001 Census Report of Assam, Directorate of Census Operation, Assam.

Education and Literacy

When compared with the neighbouring district of Sylhet, the progress in education in the district will took insignificant during the period preceding Independence. Until very recently, the Cachar consisted of Silchar, Hailakandi and North Cachar Hills Sub-divisions. In 1952, N. C. Hills was taken out from the Cachar district and was made a part of the united Mikir and North Cachar Hills district.

In the year 1856-57, there was not a single school in the district. In 1861 there was an unaided school, which had only 13 pupils. In such situation, the area constituting the Cachar was very naturally backward in literacy. Literate and educated people when required had to be brought from outside, besides a very few locals who could read and write. The matter slowly began to improve more than three decades after advent of the British rule. In 1865-66, there were only seven schools in existence. Little progress was made George Campbell's measures of reform began to take effect. In 1900-1901, there were 248 primary schools and four secondary schools in existence. Most of the people acquired literacy from schools or at home There were no literacy drives before the advent of British rule. A few Kachari kings and members of nobility were fairly educated. They had some educated employees also. But the literacy rate of common people was very low or almost nil. There were a few big landholders and people of priestly class who were at least literate if not educated. In 1903-04, there were 230 lower primary schools for boys and 238 lower primary schools for girls. There were 11 upper primary schools which were attended by 126 boys and 60 girls (Government of Assam 2004).

But even before the government undertook the task of spreading literacy and education, a Welsh Presbyterian Missionary, William Pryse, had devoted himself to it. He reached Cachar in 1851 from Sylhet. In 1856, in accordance with the advice of Captain Verner, the Government Agent for Cachar, a school was opened at Silchar with Pryse's helper

Mr Thaison being appointed in charge. In December 1863, Pryse was able to get a grant of Rs 60/- per month. Pryse paid attention to Cachar district. In his letters to the Directors, he disclosed his plan of travelling of the Hills and Cachar and to locate a youth who was still a student to maintain surveillance until the others were led voluntarily to take up and spread the teachings and the gospel of the mission by October 1886. He wrote that the missionaries were trying to establish a mission school at Barkhala about nine miles from Silchar. An old revered gentleman who was the last of the Chief Ministers of Govinda Chandra, the last king of Cachar, gifted the school. The school, now Higher Secondary School named after King Govinda Chandra still at Borkhala where of the mission

Thus, the spread of literacy in Cachar began with the missionary efforts to spread formal education. However, the efforts were concentrated in the urban areas. The present literacy status in the valley is shown in Table 2.9.

The data in Table 2.9 show that Cachar and Karimjanj districts have litaracy in slightly more than two thirds of the Barak Valley population where as in Hailakandi district total literacy covers three fifths of the population.

People of this region have had keen desire for education since long past. Consequently one fined many renowned scholars and dignitaries in the past and present. Facilities for education from primary school to University level are available here. Assam University, National Institute of Technology (NIT), Medical College, Polytechnic College, Technical School, Agricultural Training School, L.P, M.V, H.S Schools and Colleges, B.Ed Colleges and Basic Training Centers and Research Centers serve the purpose of education.

Economy

Barak Valley is now a full-fledged region having all the avenues of further prosperity. River Barak, Kushiara and Longai with their tributaries and branches facilitate navigation to carry

Table 2.9: Total Literacy in Barak Valley

District	Sex				Total	%
	Male	%	Female	%		
Cachar	481106	50.3	35,4782	50.25	1442141	48.25
Karimganj	317584	33.2	241928	33.30	1003678	33.58
Hailakandi	157474	16.5	109435	15.45	45422978	18.17
Total	9,56,164	100.0	7,06,145	100.0	29,88797	100.0

Source: Govt. of India 2001 Census Report of Assam, Directorate of Census Operation, Assam

fruits and forest products from interior parts to the markets. Railways and roadways are spread in this region. Hill section of railways and Badarpur-Shillong-Guwahati road are the linklines to connect it with the rest of the country. One airport is also available. The Hindustan Paper Mill located at Panchgram is one of the biggest paper mills in Asia. Its raw materials i.e. bamboos are grown in plenty in the region. Radio and TV centers have been functioning here since long time.

The economic condition of the people is at par with other regions of the country. Business is flourishing day by day. The region maintains a good cultural heritage in folksongs, dances etc. The valley is no doubt resource-rich, but is also one of the country's most thickly populated areas. Its forest products, water resources, fruits and sugarcane yielding potential have to be utilized. Being a land-scarce area it needs appropriate planning and technology to ensure maximum yield. Flanked by five of the seven political units in the region, its central situation has to be recognized by the Union Government for the location of the regional offices. The feeling of neglect and discrimination has to be removed and the linguistic and cultural identity of the people have to be guaranteed since these are essentially linked with the question of development (Statistical Abstracts 1960).

Literature and Culture

Literary and cultural tradition of this valley deserves special attention. From the region of the Cachari rulers, Bengali language and literature started its journey. An article written by Biswatosh Choudhury titled 'Barak Upatyakai Bangla Sahitya' provides some ideas about the new western awakening in the field of literature and the contribution of Ramkumar Nandy. And then information about awakening and the age of Shikshasebak was found. This was published in the souvenir of the All India Bengali Literary Conference held at Silchar in 1989 (Choudhury 1989).

Among the recent researchers various works by Amalendu Bhattacharjee provide a detailed picture of the evolution of literary and cultural tradition in Barak Valley in the contemporary time. Particular mention needs to be made of the following contributions by Bhattacharjee.

(i) "Language and literature of Barak Valley" paper presented in the National Seminar on ' History and Society of Barak Valley held in Delhi November 11, 1992)

(ii) Barak Upatyakay Bagla Sahita Charchsar Dharabahik Itihaas' Aksharbritta, Vol III, IInd special issue, Karim-ganj, 1993.

Among the Bengali literary figures in Cachar, during the British period, Ramkumar Nandy Mazumdar (1831-1904) made notable contributions to the valley's literary traditions.

Amalendu Bhattacharjee and Jahar Kanti Sen have discussed in detail the life and literary activities of Ramkumar Nandy Mazumdar in their "Introduction" to the Nandy's book Birangana Patrattar Kabya (Mazumdar Nandy 1997).

In another 'Introduction' to the edited volume of Ramkumar Nandy Mazumdar's 'Malinir Upakhyan', Amalendu Bhattachajee presents some additional information on the particular literary work of Ramkumar Nandy Mazumdar and also on the literary trends in Cachar during the British period (Bhattachajee 1991).

A booklet in Bengali entitled 'Amader Bai Amader Patra Patrika' published by the Barak Upatyaka Banga Sahita O Sanskriti Sammelan in 1988 provides with a complete list of all the books published from Cachar including those ones published prior to 1947. This list gives the name of novels and other literary works published during the pre-Independence phase of modern literature in Barak Valley.

Bijay Choudhury in his article 'Atit Silcharer Siksha – Sahitya Sankriti' highlights the education, literature and cultural development of Silchar. In this article gives a clear picture of the young generation in the literary and cultural field during the pre-independence period (Choudhury 1994).

With the beginning of the process of urbanization in Cachar cultural activities in and around the Silchar town started gathering momentum. Parimal De in her article "Nagarik Manan O Adunikatar Unmesh: Silchar Saharer Sanskriti Charchai Swadhinata Kayak Dashak" focused on the cultural development of Silchar town during pre-Independence period. It is a fact that written documents on this aspect is very limited. So, she interviewed some senior citizens of this town and she wrote the article. From this one gets a vivid picture of the state of culture in Silchar town during pre-independence period.

For literature and culture, though primary sources are not sufficient, the document successive census reports from 1872 onwards available in National Library, Annexed Calcutta and the records preserved in Cachar District Records Room in Silchar give us a good deal of information regarding various aspects of social history of Barak Valley. Apart from these, various books and articles written by well known scholars furnish a rich body of information about social scenario of the region.

In sum, the Barak valley is a distinct region not only in India but also in Assam itself. It is the region of biological, geographical and cultural diversities which is very much true to the variegated character of North-Eastern region as a whole. when one looks at demographic, social and cultural character, it appears the distinct one within the North East. A very high growth and destiny of population, in-migration, multi-ethnic groups, multi-lingual and multi-religious population, increasing literacy rate, multiple cultural activities, most peaceful place in the North-Eastern, growing trade activities and literacy and journalistic activities make the region different from the rest.

REFERENCES

Allen, B.C. *Assam District Gazetters*, Vol-I.

Barkataki, S. 1969 *Assam*, New Delhi: National Book Trust.

Bhattacharjee, Amalendu 1991 *Barak Upatakar Sahityer Itihaaas Rachana*. Prasanga, Swarannika, Matri Utsav, Dishari.

Bhattacharjee, J. B. 1986 Studies in The History of North-East India Shillong: Publication.

Choudhury Bijay 1994 Atit Silcharer Shiksha Sahitaya Sanskriti. Swarannika, Maitri Utsav, Silchar:Dishari.

Choudhury Dutta Mondira 2002 Impact of Modernization on the Traditional Institute of the Barmans of the Barak Valley : 1947-1990, A PhD Thesis Silchar: Assam University.

Gosh M John 1986 Topography of Assam, Delhi : Logos Press.

Goswami, P.J, 1991 Tribals in Transition,Guwahati: Government of Assam.

Government of Assam 1960 Statistical Abstracts of Assam, Directorate of Economics and Statistics, Guwahati

Government of Assam 2003 *Statistical Handbook of Assam*, Directorate of Economics and Statistics, Guwahati

Government of Assam 2004 *Statistical Handbook of Assam*, Directorate of Economics and Statistics, Guwahati

Government of India 1991 Census of India: Assam, Guwahati : Directorate of Census Operation, Assam

Government of India 2001 Census of India: Assam, Guwahati : Directorate of Census Operation, Assam

Government of India 1951 Census of India,Vol-12, Part-V, Assam, Manipur, Tripura and Shillong

Government of India 1961 Assam District Census Handbook, Cachar District, p-12

Government of India 1971 Census of India: Assam, Guwahati: Directorate of Census Operation, Assam

Government of India 1981 Census of India: Assam, Guwahati: Directorate of Census Operation, Assam

Hunter,W. W. 1982 Statistical Account of Assam

Kamaluddin Ahmed 1998 'Bangiya Chatunder Shataki Surma Barak' Satabdir Taitapunjee, Barak Upataka Banga Sahitya O Sanskriti Sammelon. Prasongik Printers : Silchar

Mazumdar Nandy, Ramkumar 1997 Malinir Upakhayan, Calcutta: Ratna Prakasan

Mazumdar, A 1996 Statistical People of Barak Valley and An Agenda For Research on Valley's Economy, North-Eastern Centre For Advanced Studies. Silchar:

Nath, R. M. 1981 Antiquities of Cachar, Silchar.

Ratan T 1990 Encyclopedia of North East India Delhi:Kalpaz Publication.

Roy, Janmajit 1991 Barak Upatakaya Sahitya Charcha Ek Bismrita Adhayai, Aksharbritta, Silchar.

3

Press in the Historical Perspective

Press is a social product that has a long history of its evolution along with social developments. It developed as a product of the modern world, particularly the western world where modern science and capitalism emerged and spread all over the world. But the roots of press are found in the ancient Rome of the western world and even before that in China of the oriental world. Like many other remarkable developments, the press also has its moorings for technological, ideological and sociological growth in the industrial and political revolution, democracy, capitalism and modern culture in the western world. To understand the origin, growth and development of the press in Barak valley one needs to look into the general trends of the historical emergence of the press in general and in India in particular. Tho present chapter is therefore devoted to take a historical stock of the press in society.

Ancient Origin

The history of newspaper goes back to 59 B.C in Rome with the publication of daily events in the form of bulletin known as 'Act Diruna'. It was put up in a public place for all to read. China also has a long distinguished tradition in bringing out newspaper. More than 2000 years before Christ, China had a newspaper in which news was composed in verse and chanted in streets for public hearing. The earliest example of modern newspaper is also found in China. It was essentially a court journal that appeared about 500 A.D (Ghosh 1991). The first regularly published newspapers appeared in German cities and in Antwerp around 1609 AD. The 'English Mercuric' known to be the first English newspaper was published in the regime of Queen Elizabeth. One of the first daily newspapers 'The Daily Courant' was brought out in English in 1702 by Elizabeth Mallet, a lady from London (Bose 1979).

The Growth in the Modern World

The seventeenth century witnessed the establishment of the technical and administrative framework of newspapers in Europe. The eighteenth century went on to create the newspaper in its complete form with daily publications and miscellaneous contents. The progress of journalism was speeded up by the development of party system in Government. Parties emerged at the very time when the newspaper appeared to be a force in the political and social affairs of the people. A noteworthy fact in the early days of news publication was that it began with a description of events across immense geographical areas and did not confine itself to a small local area. As one writer puts it:

> "In the societies of Europe, it planted in the mind of individual literate citizen the picture of world of public events which he never see or experience for himself. It placed his own society within the context, the continent and the world" (Parthasarthy 1989).

The eighteenth century saw the emergence of greater writers and journalists like Daniel Defoe, (author of Robinson Crusoe), Jonathan Swift (Gulliver's Travel), and Henry Fielding. Among them Defoe was probably the most important English journalist of the time. He printed and edited the weekly 'Review'. According to the one writer,

> "the literacy of the early 18th century was not the only one to find journalism both interesting and profitable, many other later novelists, essayists even play writers and poets have been found to write for newspapers and to call themselves journalists and over the years they helped to raise the standard of writing and reporting often to great heights" (Smith 1979).

Journalism emerged gradually with regularity of publication. When the postal services, printing capacity and supply of materials were all sufficiently and consistently developed to the point at which the appearance of a journal as a weekly, tri-weekly or daily could be assured, journalism could be said to have come into existence. By the end of 18th century, England was flooded with newspaper reading rooms, each subscribing up to four score newspapers. John Doherty, a radical reformer, operated a 'Coffee and News' in Manchester which opened at 6 o' clock in the morning and remained open till late night with the *"most able and popular publication of the day, whether political, literary or scientific available in a comfortable gentle apartments"*.

The able houses purchased newspapers to attract customer were earlier an inn would charge for the right to read them.

In 1878 AD the Anti-Jacobin (a newspaper) had 2500 subscribers but claimed a readership between 17500 and 50,000. At that time the press was more active instrument of propaganda than the platform. William Coblett was among the earliest to exploit the medium of print to build up a radical mass opinion dedicated to dismantling the oligarch political machinery surviving from the previous century. According to one historian, the 18th century newspaper had been synonymous with the political bribery and journalistic scurrility. It was normal for editors to charge 'insertion' and contradiction fees', 'a polite euphemism' for a system by which anyone could print attacks on his enemies at the price of an advertisement and his enemy pay the editor for the opportunity to return them in kind. Even John Walter I, founder of the 'Daily

Universal Register' (later 'The Times ') made money by this means (Parthasarthy 1989).

By the Beginning of 19th century, important advances were made in the technique of journalism and the production of newspaper. A remarkable advancement was the systematic reporting of speeches and debates. The advent of shorthand writing transformed the art of reporting into a science. 'Shorthand', as one writer observed, was the first of that long series of journalistic techniques, which, at first, seemed to promise the reader the complete recovery of some semblance of reality. It was the promised ability to recover the dimension of reality in reporting that turned it into an occupation. A competent shorthand reporter seemed to have acquired an almost supernatural power and shorthand was invested with the same kind of social optimism as the microphone and television camera in later times (Smith 1979). Thus, it gave the reporter an aura of neutrality as he stood between event and reader.

The newspaper of the mid to late 19th century consisted of a very large measure of shorthand reporters. The discovery of the telegraph and telegram created further demarcations in the newspaper. Reporting from more than one place became easier though much more expensive. As one writer remarks:

> "the telegraph created most certainly a global village but it raised more issues than it resolved when readers troubled to ask themselves whether they were being given a complete and balanced account. The telegraph created a pressure world within journalism. It made possible the idea that a daily newspaper should encompass all the events and of the day. Henceforth, daily journalism operated within new tense, as it was instantaneous present" (Grey 1968).

The advent of news agencies helped speed up the process of supply of news from all parts of the world. The first Englishman to news agency was Thomas Phelippes in the Elizabethan era. Among the first to work on a large commercial scale was Charles Haves, a rich Portuguese merchant, who ran a new bureau in France in the first half of the 19th century. His contemporary Bernhard Wolff, a German Jewish Physician, with a strong interest in money market, started a news service in Burling. Another competitor who beat them all to stay in the field was Paul Julies Reuter's. Reuter, born in Germany, set up his news agency in a small room in Paris only with his wife to assist him. The invention of telegraph provided Reuters with a splendid opportunity and he opened small telegraph office at Achen in Holland to supply bankers and merchants with financial information. As more and more telegraph line opened, his business expanded. By 1860 AD he established himself as a chief supplier of foreign news to almost every newspaper and periodical in Britain. One of his most famous scoops was assassination of President, Abram Lincoln, of United States in 1865 AD (Parthasarthy 1989).

The 1880s and 1890s were the golden age of journalism in England, Europe and USA. Public opinion appeared to become the primary force by which society moved and its miraculous dynamism was the end product of newspaper. W.T. Stead who was the editor of 'Pall Mall ' Gazette and later of the Times pioneered the 'New journalism 'of England in 1880s and prepared the way for the mass newspaper of the 20th century. Mr. Stead wrote that:

> "the telegraph and printing press together had converted Britain into a Vast Agora or Assembly of the whole community in which the discussion of the affairs of the state is carried on from day to day in the hearing of the whole people"(Grey 1968).

The American Journalism

Across the Atlantic Ocean in the United States in the early 18th century, the American colonies presented all the preconditions for the rapid growth of newspaper industry. The first American newspaper was printed in Boston on April 24, 1704. Its editor and publisher was postmaster John Campbell. It was called the 'Boston Newsletter'.

A new era in the American journalism began on September 3, 1833 with the publication of 'The New York Sun' by Benjamin H. Day. It was printed on four pages, each about two third of the area of the modern tabloid pages. On September 18, 1851, the world's greatest newspaper, the 'New York Times' was born. Its publishers were Henry J. Raymond and Jorge Jones. At the turn of the 20th century, the American newspaper was able to produce well over 100 pages in some of their issues. From1910, colour printing became possible and colour was extensively used in display advertising. Today, in America the traditional definition of newspaper is being modified and expanded to accommodate changes in society, reader-demands and new technology. Modern newspapers in terms of printing and publishing have reached stupendous proportions with the advent of the electronic era. In 1820 printing of a newspaper was a hazardous job and posed many problems. Before 1860 newspaper were being produced through single stamped sheet. An American inventor, Richard Heo, in 1840, developed the first version of the rotary press. He found a way to fit the printed type round a cylinder, which was then linked to automatic roller, while four smaller cylinders brought the sheets of paper into contact with it. The lion type machine, which revolutionized printing, was not in the market until 1892. It was originally made by Ottoman Mergenthaler, a German emigrant to America. However, the problem of printing was simultaneously solved by Hippeyte Marinioni who demonstrated his advanced rotatory press in the Paris Exhibition in 1869. This model turned the roll of paper back on its path enabling successive sheets of any size to be printed on both sides and then cut and folded into piles of complete newspaper with great speed (Parthasarthy 1989).

With the rapid expansion, technological development and spread of literacy, newspaper grew in popularity and demand of printers gradually discovered that they could count roughly on a certain number of buyers for each issue. The concept of circulation was thus born, suggesting a profitable enterprise with further increase in sales until it became a big business in the 20th century. But technological, geographical and transportational barriers hindered the growth of press till the end of 19th century. The press as it exists today is the outcome of a historical process in which many individuals participated without foreseeing what the ultimate product of their efforts was to be. Newspapers have continued to grow and change in their own incalculable ways.

In sum, the press has travelled long through the history from east to west. It is the atmosphere of the new world that gave a spurt and momentum to the development of the press in Europe. Ultimately, the social conditions of the society in USA contributed a great leap forward of the press in the modern world.

REFERENCES

Ahuja, B.N 1998 *Mass Communication,* New Delhi: Allied Publishers.

and Relevance, New Delhi: Kanishka Publishers and Distributors.

Apte, Mahadeb L 1978 *Mass Culture, Language and Arts, In India,* Bombay: Popular Prakashan.

Basu, Jitendra 1979 *Romance of Indian Journalism* Calcutta: Calcutta University Press

Bhatt, C.S. 1997 *Indian Press 1955,* New Delhi: Publication Division, Ministry of Information & Broadcasting, Govt. of India.

Ghosh, Subir 1991 *Mass Media Today,* Calcutta: Profile Publisher

Kumar, J. Keval 1981 *Mass Communication in India,* Mumbai:Jaico Publishing House.

Mankekar, R.D 1973 *The Press under Pressure,* New Delhi: Indian Book Company

Mehta, D.S. 1979 *Mass Communication and Journalism in India,* New Delhi: Allied Publishers.

Murthy, Krishna Nadig 1966 *Indian Journalism,* Mysore *'Prasaranga'*:University of Mysore.

Natrajan,S, 1962 *History of Press in India,* Bombay: Popular Prakashan

Nayar, Kuldeep 1977 *The Judgment,* New Delhi: Vikas Publishing House.

Padhya, S.K 1991 *Battle of Freedom of the Press in India* New Delhi: Academic Foundation.

Padhya, S.K and Sahu, N.R. 1997 *The Press In India - Perspective in Development*

Parthasarathy, Rangaswami 1989 *Journalism in India- From the Earliest Time to the Present Day,* New Delhi: Sterling Publishers Pvt. Ltd.

Rau Chalapathi, M 1968 *The Press in India,* New Delhi: Allied Publishers Pvt Ltd.

Rau Chalapathi, M 1980 *200 Years of Indian Press, Vidura:* February.

4

The Indian Press

The Emergence

In ancient India what the king did, his laws and actions against citizens and generally his achievements formed the staple diet of news. News was given in inscription on walls of temples and on copper plates and through victory coins and writings on rocks. There were government officials who by the beat of drum gathered the populace and announced the policies and decisions of the king or government. The king who met his ministers and commander-in-chief daily at a *durbar* gathered news of what was happening in his kingdom and abroad from his counselors who were expected to be fully informed of events and public opinion. According to the tradition the very first question the king asked to his prime minister at the *durbar* was "well, Prime Minister what is the news today?" Indeed, news was communicated at that time by words of mouth. Kings and noblemen had their own sources of news. Wandering minstrels acting as a 'correspondents' moved from one royal court to another, picking up news of battles won or lost. They gathered useful information for courtiers and merchants. They also embroidered their news to make a good story as the reporters of today do.

In India newsletters containing general information of the royal court or extraordinary events from the provinces were in circulation during the Moghul Rule. But this was not for general people. It was available only to a group of nobles. The printing process was brought to India in the 16th century by Christian Missionaries. The British also brought printing press India augmenting the efforts of the Missionaries. Initially, the pioneers of journalism in India were English men. In India the first newspaper in the modern sense was the 'Bengal 'Gazette' or 'Calcutta General Advertiser' which made its appearance on 29th January 1780. It was edited and published by James Augustus Hickey. It was a weekly newspaper well known as 'Hickey's Gazette'. Hickey's paper was exclusively meant for the Britishers and never took into consideration the aspiration of the local population. The Indian community was unable to join. It took another 38 years before a newspaper in Indian language was published by an Indian, reflecting the ups and downs of the Indian society. The credit goes to Ganga Kishor Battacharjee, a teacher with reformist ideas. As the first Indian to bring out a newspaper, he has perhaps a greater claim as to be called the 'Papa of the Indian Press'. The weekly paper known as the 'Bengal Gazette' was published sometime between May 12 and May 18 in 1818 AD (Ghosh 1991).

The Christian missionaries and European editors have left indelible imprints in the history of Indian journalism. Although their primary aim was to enlighten their fellow Europeans, they covertly reached the educated Indians and thus opened up a new vista of knowledge. As Nadig Krishna Mutrhy has written:

> "Almost all the European editors were pro-British and naturally they attempted to play down the nationalist movement for freedom in their newspaper columns. Some of them did believe in freedom of the press, but had little opportunity to express their opinion under the circumstance then prevailing. Some of them were staunch supporters of the regime and advocated the suppression of the Indian movement vigorously. Apart from this, the European editors laid a firm foundation and great tradition for Indian journalism to develop it on modern lines. They

were the first to utilize technological innovation. They really had a fervent belief in journalistic ethics and most of them practised them. Even the education in journalism owes its origin in India to Europeans. Dr. Annie Besant, the founder of the Home Rule Movement, started the first journalism course in 1920 at Madras. Her 'New India' newspaper became a practical centre for journalism training" (Nadig K. Murthy 1980).

During the Period from AD 1818 to AD 1857, there was rapid growth of Vernacular press in Bengal. Apart from the newspapers and periodicals owned by the European missionaries, leading Bengalis also came forward to edit papers of their own. Indian-owned English newspapers and periodicals also emerged in other parts of India apart from Bengal. The Bengali press had a head start and attained maturity faster than the language press in other parts of India. But during AD 1818 to AD 1857, there was also a growth of various Indian language papers. This was facilitated by the efforts of Christian missionaries as well as the Indian reformers. And finally politically consciousness had already struck roots in India before AD 1857 and one of the stirking trends of the Indian awakening was the growth of political movement. Leading to broader nationalist movement in the latter half of the 19th century, the rapid growth of the press and the growth of political consciousness were inter linked (Neogi 1997).

In the pre-rebellion (1857) period, the urge for socio-religious reforms and cultural advancement seems to be more urgent and necessary prerequisite for social upliftment of the Indians. The growth of political consciousness was at a slow pace. However, it owed much to the growth of press, particularly the vernacular press. The exploitative nature of the British rule was thoroughly exposed; protesting voices rose against the repressive measures of the Government and nationalist ideas were spread among the educated Indians. The role of press in India's struggle for Independence was even more glorious and active in next ninety years. Between 1818 AD and 1857 AD, there appeared many dailies, weeklies, bi-weeklies and monthlies published from Bengal. The Bengali papers included “Sambad Kumudi”, “Samachar Chandrika”, “Sambad Prabhakar”, “Jnananvesan”, etc. The first Hindi weekly ‘Oodunta Martand’ (1826) and first Hindi daily, ‘Samachar Sudha Varshan’ (1854), appeared from Calcutta. The first English Journal ‘Satyadoota’ was published from Bellary in 1836 AD by the missionaries. The first Oriya paper ‘Jnanaruna’ came out in AD 1849. The first Tamil paper was ‘Tamil Magazine’ which appeared in AD 1832. The first Kannada paper ‘Kannada Samacher’ appeared in AD 1832. The Malaya-lam newspaper ‘Vignayana Nikshepam’ appeared in 1840. The Marathi newspaper made its appearance in AD 1822 followed by so many Gujarati papers like ‘Bombay Darpan’, ‘Prabakar’, ‘Vartaman Dipika’, etc. (Neogi 1997) It is to be noted that most of the ventures were patronized by the Christian missionaries (Ahuja 1998).

The pioneer of the Indian language journalism was the Serompore Missionaries with ‘Samachar Doran’ and other Bengali periodical and Raja Ram Mohan Ray with his Persian newspaper ‘Miratool Akbar’ (Kumar 1981). By 1821, there were nine newspapers in Bengali and one in Persian, all published from Bengal. The first Hindi newspaper came out in 1826 from Calcutta. In course of only another fourteen years, newspapers in most of the major languages like Tamil (1831), Telugu (1893), Marathi (1832), Urdu (1836), Malayalam (1840) were published, reflecting the growing social and political awareness of the Indians.

The Pre-Independence Indian Press

The history of Indian press covers a long span of about two hundred years during which it struggled against social and political evils. It has glorious history with an important role in the freedom movement when it faced persecution. In the post-Independence period it has served as a staunch upholder of democratic principles and powerful agent of social change. The overall Indian press experience is best looked at within this kind of context because it highlights the strength and qualitative effects or the weakness and frailties of the general developing society, which must not be underplayed (Murty 1980).

The history of Indian journalism in the pre-Independence period can be classified in following phases :

The **Phase of 1780-1818** constitutes some kind of a preparatory phase, marked by the contributions of William bolts, James Augustus Hicky and others.

The **Phase of 1818-1868** includes contribution of silk Buckingham, the inspiring efforts of Raja Ram Mohan Roy, the struggle against censorship, harassment, deportation and persecution, the struggle to establish some measure of freedom expression, the dilemmas of colonial rulers, the interesting responses to the press question by Bentick and Metcalfe (the Liberator), the establishment of the pro-Raj Times of India and the big impact on the political and intellectual mood of the first war of Indian Independence (Pandey 1999).

The **Phase of the period of 1868-1919** witnessed the rise of Indian press as part of the nationalist or anti-imperialist struggle and the manifestation of two tendencies in the press. The one is the support to the colonial Raj and its policies; the other is a line of criticism and opposition. This stage sees major technological developments such as the opening of the telegraph line (1851) in Calcutta, the appearance of the railway and the completion of the land telegraph line from England to India. During this phase, Indian press comes into its own. Some notable events in this respect are the founding of the 'Amrit Bazar Patrika' (1868) and the 'Hindu' (1876) with the pro-raj newspapers. 'The Statesman', also appeared in 1875. The founding of the Indian National Congress in 1885 reminds us that the history of the patriotic Indian press pre-dates the history of Indian party politics. This period witnesses the "Sedition" trials of Tilak (1897 and 1908), the return of Mahatma Gandhi to India (1915) and the struggle against the Rowllet Act and against uncivilized colonial repression. Tilak and Ghandhi, themselves journalists, wielded a major influence on the field. The Jalianwala Bagh massacre closes this stage, with the press divided sharply into that section which condemns the crime and outrage, and the opposition camp which defends or provides apologies for (Bhatt 1997).

The **Phase of 1919-1937** sees the differentiation of the Indian press into "moderate" and 'radical' tendencies in relation to the strategy and tactics of the freedom movement. The struggle between the nationalist and pro-British press continues. The 'Sedition' trails of Gandhi in 1922 witnesses a heroic response. In Britain, the first Labour Government is formed and new attitudes to the Indian questions were shaped and expressed. In India, nationalist newspaper such as "The Hindustan Times" and the "Indian Express" were established while those already established make impressive progress in their reach and influence. The struggle for the freedom of the press and for wider civil liberties acquired a full voice.

The **Phase of the period 1937- 1947** sees the maturing and assertive tendencies in the press and significant professional developments such as the news service, the pooling of arrangements and the expanded coverage of foreign news.

In pre-Independence era, the Indian language journalism took its birth with the experience of English journalism behind it. Raja Ram Mohan Roy was the founder and father of Indian language journalism. As a fighter for the rights of women, a social reformer with refined standards, the founder of Brahma Samaj, and a father of language journalism he will be remembered for all times to come in the pages of Indian history.

On November 1, 1858, Queen Victoria took charge of the administration of India. To maintain a better relationship between the press and the Government, Lord Canning, who continued to be the British representative in India, established the 'Editors Room' where the journalists had an access to come and examine the Government papers relating to public interest. From 1858 AD onwards, the sale of both English and Indian newspaper went up. The Indian language newspapers were vehement and strong in their criticisms of Governments policies and actions. The Vernacular Press Act IX of 1878 became law in March 1878 and the language press all over the India was muzzled (Basu 1979). This act was great blow to the freedom of the press in India, which caused the language newspapers to suffer drastically.

The 'Hindu', an English newspaper, was started as a weekly on 20th September 1876 from Madras. It was converted into a tri-weekly in 1883 to create a political awareness among the people (Padhy 1997). The birth of the Indian National Congress heralded a new era in the history of Indian journalism. The Indian National Congress was born under the leadership of an Englishman A.O. Hume in 1885. Towards the end of 19th century, for the first time, a conference of editors and journalists was held in Calcutta. In 1891, 'The Native Press Association" was founded with an objective to improve the tone on native press (Padhy 1997).

During the World War I, Indian press wholeheartedly supported the cause of the Allied Powers and lent a helping hand to Great Britain. In return the Indians wanted freedom and independence. A new national group called the Home Rule League inspired and encouraged by Anne Besant and Bal Gangadhar Tilak emerged on the Indian political scene. Annie Besant and Tilak both were genius journalists of high reputation. Mahatma Gandhi after returning to India from South Africa in 1915 took the charge of Indian freedom movement. He was not new to journalism. He published a newspaper called 'Indian Opinion'. He acquired an English and Gujarati weekly to spread his ideas. He took over "Young India" in 1919 from Jamunadas, Dwarkadas of Bombay and also started a Gujarati weekly, **Navajivan** (Parthasarthy 1991) Articles written by Gandhiji covered most crucial issues like Hindu-Muslim unity, abolitions of liquor and wine, promotion of khadi and village industry, removal of untouchability, etc. (Moitra 1969).

During the struggle for Independence, the need of national language daily was very much felt by the leaders for propagating the view of the Indian National Congress. So, on 5th September 1920, the 'Aj' was born. Started by Shiv Prasad Gupta, it was a nationalist independent paper and whole heartedly supported the views of the Congress It is to be mentioned here that the newspapers' freedom was curbed by a number of press acts and ordinances. As a result, most of them suffered in terms of publication and circulation. Many nationalist newspapers which were publishing nationalist views suffered a lot and stopped publication (Padhy 1997).

The Post-Independence Indian Press

The year 1947 brought Independence to India and heralded a new era in the history of Indian press. It witnessed not only the opening of a new chapter in its history but also saw the emergence of press with a role to play with much vigour and energy. Before Independence the role was to support the cause of national Independence. But after the Independence its role has become much more difficult and significant as it has to address itself to the task of national development and nation-building. It acquired a new dimension in both make-up and content. The scenario has completely changed in respect of publication and circulation (Natrajan 1962).

A press commission was appointed in September 1952 under the chairmanship of Justice Rajadhyaksha. The commission submitted its report in 1954 recommending the establishment of press council. The press council was established by an act of parliament in 1965. Its first president was Justice N. Rajagopal Iyengar. The Press Council Act was repealed in January 1976 during the Emergency and the council was re-established under the Press Council Act of 1978 (Pandey 1999).

The Second Press Commission was set up in May 1978 under the chairmanship of Justice P.K. Goswami. The commission was reconstituted in April 1980 under chairmanship of Justice K.K. Mathew

The declaration of emergency in June 1975 by the government of Prime Minister Indira Gandhi came as a shocking blow to the Indian press which was its greatest victim. The Government suppressed transmission of news from one place to another by imposing censorship on newspapers. The underground newspapers were however active. More than 30 presses were seized and over 7000 people were arrested in connection with the publication and circulation of underground literature (Kumar 1981). However, all the restrictions were removed by the Janata Government which came to power in 1977 and Indian press once again breathed freedom.

The evolution of the Indian press from the obscure beginning in East India Company up to present time has striking features of its own. Equally significant has been the development of the press on the technical side. When country attained Independence, the days of professional and with a missionary ardour gradually reduced. The character of newspaper ownership changed fast. The newspaper proprietors evinced keenness in building up commercial position. As a result group newspaper, chain publication and trust publication emerged with a new control of newspaper readership (Kumar 1998).

In the post-Independence period, to cope up with increased circulation it was found necessary to become self sufficient in the matter of paper. This was done by starting factories in India. Newsprint shortage gave an impetus to new industry to manufacture newsprint in India. The Nepa mills at Nepanagar near Nagpur started production in 1956 with a production capacity of 120 tons per day (Murthy 1966). With the phenomenal rise in circulation advertisement revenue multiplied. The high profits enabled many papers to build up large resources which were used for expanding and modernizing their technical equipment. Latest machineries were placed and with their installation, a striking improvement in the quality of Indian newspaper production took place. As Dr. Nadik Krishna Murthi observed:

> "Gradually the newspaper curved for more effective professional techniques and conveniences. Provision was made for better opportunities for special correspondence at home and abroad."

Feature writing which was hardly an activity of Indian journalism got an impetus. Encouragement was given personalized columns. This helped columnist to shine and the time was ripe for individual triumphs. Eminent journalists like B. Shiva Rao, Pothan Joseph, Durga Das, N Raghunath Iyer, Khasa Subba Rao, M Chalipathi Rau, S Gopal Swami, Krishnalal Sridharini, H. Vankatasubbiah and Frank Moraes achieved destination in various ways in the Indian newspaper world with their sparkling bi-lined columns. Besides the columnist writing in English, there were numerous other equally famous columnists in almost all the Indian language newspapers who popularized columns through their facile pen. Journalistic rank expanded itself and administrative improvements were also effective inside. The newspapers became better organized and were now systematically managed (Murthy 1966: 115-16).

The most remarkable development after Independence was the formation of the Press Trust of India (PTI) in 1949. The PTI is still the biggest nationwide newspaper agency. The PTI has longest tele-printer link in India and is one of the biggest news agencies in Asia. The PTI was founded with a view to raise the status of the members of profession of journalism and to maintain the highest standard of professional contact. Another significant development was formation of Audit Bureau of Circulation in 1980 to guarantee the circulation of each of its member publications. The certificate regarding circulation issued by A.B.C. is accepted at face value all over the world.

Present Status of Indian Press

The press adds 34 million readers in the last 2 years. Press continues to grow, adding 21 million readers between 2002 and 2005. Over the last three years the number of readers of dailies and magazines put together among those aged 15 years and above has grown from 179 mn to 200 mn – a growth of 4% every year.

There is still significant scope for growth as 314 million people who can read and understand any language do not read any publication. It is not just affordability that is a constraint, since 21 million of these literate non-readers belong to the upscale (NRS 2005).

There are nearly as many rural readers as urban readers. Of the 200 mn readers as many as 98 mn are from rural India and 101 mn from urban India. (NRS 2005).

Newspapers add substantially to the reader base. The reader base for dailies/newspapers increased from 155 mn in 2002 to 176 mn this year – an increase of nearly 14% over three years. However, the growth in reach of dailies is less than the literacy growth of 21% in the same period. (NRS 2005).

The highest read Hindi Daily in India now surpasses a readership of 21 mn. A list of top 10 dailies and magazines in Table 4.1 shows that as many as 7 of the top 10 dailies have consistently improved their rankings in the last three years.

Table 4.2 shows a list of top ten dailies as per NRS 2005

Dainik Jagran has taken the top slot even though the previous year's No. 1 Dainik Bhaskar has also grown handsomely. This is because the number of literates in UP, Bihar and Jharkhand (strong Dainik Jagran markets) has grown explosively - while Dainik Bhaskar has not been as fortunate in its strong markets.

Decline of Audience for Magazines

Table 4.3 shows the top ten magazines in rural India as per NRS 2005.

Table 4.4 displays the top ten magazines in urban India as per the NRS 2005

Table 4.3 and Table 4.4 show that overall reader base of the magazines has both a declined in the reader base, both in urban and rural India. The reach of magazines has declined from 86 mn in 2002 to 69 mn in 2005. Magazines have lost 19% of their reach since 2002.

Table 4.1: Top Ten Rural Dailies (excluding Malayalam)

(Readership figures in '000s)

Publication	NRS 2002 (15+)		NRS 2003 (12+)		NRS 2005 (12+)	
	Rank	Readership	Rank	Readership	Rank	Readership
Dainik Jagran	2	12670	2	14982	1	21123
Dainik Bhaskar	1	13163	1	15709	2	17373
Eenadu	5	9277	4	9458	3	11349
Hindustan	9	6385	7	7899	4	10538
Amar Ujala	8	6431	6	8640	5	10378
Daily Thanti	4	9354	3	10094	6	9370
Lokmat	6	7840	8	7867	7	8821
Rajasthan Patrika	15	5432	11	7353	8	8628
Times Of India	12	5665	10	7419	9	8064
Anand Bazar Patrika	10	6357	13	6092	10	4215

Source : National Readership Survey, 2005, Bombay.

Table 4.2: Top Ten Urban Dailies (excluding Malayalam)

(Readership figures in '000s)

Publication	NRS 2002 (15+)		NRS 2003 (12+)		NRS 2005 (12+)	
	Rank	Readership	Rank	Readership	Rank	Readership
Dainik Jagran	2	6764	2	8494	1	10462
Dainik Bhaskar	1	7962	1	9523	2	9706
Times of India	3	5427	3	6925	3	7294
Amar Ujala	9	3829	5	4900	4	5444
Daily Thanti	5	4571	4	6177	5	5261
Lokmat	7	4185	8	4228	6	4844
Gujrat Samachar	8	3968	10	4002	7	4591
Ananda Bazar Patrika	6	4203	6	4483	8	4359
Hindusthan	13	3283	9	4009	9	4257
Eenadu	4	4902	7	4239	10	4215

Source : National Readership Survey, 2005, Bombay.

Table 4.3: Top Ten Rural Magazines (excluding Malayalam)

(Readership figures in '000s)

	NRS 2002 (15+)		NRS 2003 (12+)		NRS 2005 (12+)	
Publication	Rank	Readership	Rank	Readership	Rank	Readership
India Today (H)	4	5127	2	5900	1	10698
Saras Salil (H)	1	10608	1	9385	2	10554
India Today (E)	3	5658	7	4194	3	6254
Kungumum	40	1527	81	765	4	5571
Kumudam	7	4464	15	2887	5	4661
Sarita	18	3078	11	3423	6	4182
Grihashobha (H)	2	6050	4	5414	7	4107
Swati SVP	11	3581	19	2467	8	3953
Meri Saheli	14	3385	6	4266	9	2797
Ananda Vikatan	16	3126	31	1689	10	2741

Source : National Readership Survey, 2005, Bombay.

Table 4.4: TopTen Urban Magazines (excluding Malayalam)

(Readership figures in '000s)

Publication	NRS 2002 (15+)		NRS 2003 (12+)		NRS 2005 (12+)	
	Rank	Readership	Rank	Readership	Rank	Readership
India Today (H)	4	3404	2	4135	1	5171
India Today (E)	1	4830	3	3441	2	4779
Kungumum	4	3591	3	3330		
Grihashobha (H)	2	4405	1	4319	4	2699
Kumudam	9	2418	11	1974	5	2670
Saras Salil (H)	6	2703	5	3040	6	2142
Sarita	14	2028	9	2177	7	1957
MeriSaheli	7	2481	4	3347	8	1886
Outlook	21	1486	20	1300	9	1732
Ananda Vikatan	15	1953	23	1266	10	1681

Source : National Readership Survey, 2005, Bombay.

The time spent on press medium has increased over the years. An urban adult now spends on press and TV an average of 17 hours a week; on press 4.9 hours and TV 11.8 hours. The time spent on radio is 10 hours a week. The time spent by the average rural adult on press and TV together is 14 hours a week and that on radio is 9 hours a week (NRS 2005)

Press increases its share of urban media day. Today the average urban adult spends 42 minutes per day reading dailies and magazines and 1 hour 42 minutes watching TV. The average reading time used to be 32 minutes and the average viewing time 1 hour 40 minutes 3 years ago. Contrary to expectations, the press has increased its share of the day at the expense of TV - it accounts for 30% of the time spent, up from 24% three years ago (NRS 2005).

In sum, the modern press in India was started by the British with administrative objective. Before Independence the leaders of the Indian freedom movement contributed a lot to the English and vernacular presses in India and they used it as an effective means to propagate their message to the common people scattered far and wide in the country. After Independence the press became one of the important means of the political and intellectual leadership to disseminate the message in the masses for development and nation-building. The present status of the press indicates that it has come a long way from its humble beginning in the British Period. Now, there are as many rural readers as urban in India. The readership of magazine, especially in urban India, has shown an encouraging uptrend over the years in the contemporary times.

REFERENCES

Aggarwal, Vir Bala 1992 *Mass Media in Rural Development: Some Research Issues,*

Agree, Waren K, Ault Philip H. and Emery Edwin 1977 *Introduction to Mass Communication,* New York: Harper & Row Publishers.

Ahuja, B.N. 1998 *Mass Communication,* New Delhi: Allied Publishers.

Apte, Mahadeb L 1978 *Mass Culture, Language, Arts, In India,* Bombay: Popular Prakashan.

Bagchi Geopab and Pallab Mukhopadheya 1997 *Mass Communication and Social Development,*

Baghel, D.S. 1975 *Social Control and Social Change,* Reewa : Pushparaj Prakashan.

Basu, Jitendra 1979 *Romance of Indian Journalism,* Calcutta: Calcutta University Press

Bhargava, M 1987 *Role of Press in the Freedom Movement,* New Delhi : Reliance Publishers.

Bhatt, C.S. 1997 *Indian Press 1955,* New Delhi: Publication Division, Ministry of

Chauhan, Swasti and Chandra Nar 1985 *Journalism Today – Principles, Practices and Challenges,* New Delhi :Kanishka Publishers & Distributors.

Communicator, April – June

Communicator, December.

Ghosh, Subir 1991 *Mass Media Today,* Calcutta: Profile Publisher.

Information & Broadcasting, Govt. of India.

Joseph, Ammu 1997 Press in India-Priorities *Mainstream,* October 4.

Joseph, M.K 1996 *Modern Media and Communication, in* M.K. Joseph *Mass Media and Challenge of Change,* New Delhi: Anmol Publications Pvt. Ltd.

Kumar, J. Keval 1981 *Mass Communication in India,* Mumbai: Jaico Publishing House.

Mehta, D.S. 1979 *Mass Communication and Journalism in India,* New Delhi: Allied Publishers.

Moitra, Mohir 1969 *A History of Indian Journalism,* National Book Agency Pvt. Ltd.

Mulgaokar, M.S. 1984 *The Press in India,* Bombay: Popular Prakashan

Murthy, Krishna Nadig 1966 *Indian Journalism,* Mysore *'Prasaranga'*: University of Mysore.

National Readership Survey 2005 Bombay.

Nayar, Kuldeep 1977 *The Judgment,* New Delhi: Vikas Publishing House.

Neogi, Gautam 1977 *Role of Press in India's Struggle for Independence*:

Historical Judgment, Indian Journalists Association, Platinum Jubilee Commemoration Volume.

Padhya, S.K 1991 *Battle of Freedom of the Press in India,* New Delhi: Academic Foundation.

Padhya, S.K and Sahu, N.R. 1997 *The Press In India - Perspective in Development and Relevance,* New Delhi: Kanishka Publishers and Distributors.

Pandey, G. P. 1999 *Press and Social Change,* Delhi: Manak Publication Pvt. Ltd

Parthasarathy, Rangaswami 1989 *Journalism in India- From the Earliest Time to the Present Day,* New Delhi: Sterling Publishers Pvt. Ltd.

Rau Chalapathi, M 1968 *The Press in India,* New Delhi: Allied Publishers Pvt Ltd

Rau Chalapathi, M 1980 *200 Years of Indian Press, Vidura:* February.

5

The Press in Assam

Assamese language, the medium of vernacular journalism of Assamese people, can be traced back to the seventh century AD. It developed literary forms by 13th century Rudra Kaudalis translation of '*Dronaparva*' (of the Mahabaharata) and Madhava Kandalis rendering of the Ramayana are two works of classical eminence of the early period. The new Vaishnavite movement in the 15th century AD gave an impetus to the development of Assamese literature. Sankar Deva popularized the movement by his great poetic composition, dramas and lyrics.

Origin and Growth of the Assamese Press

The American Baptist Missionaries had a plan to enter China and to spread Christianity in that country. The American Baptist Foreign Missionary Union took keen interest in this regard. The Chinese authorities did not allow any foreigner to enter into China. So, the Baptist Missionaries cancelled their plan. In 1836, Major F. Tenkins, Commissioner of Assam wrote to Mr. Trevellyan, a civil serviceman in Bengal, inviting the Baptist Missionaries to start a station on at Sadiya., an eastern most part of Assam, now in Lohit Distt. of Arunachal Pradesh. An enthusiastic young missionary, Nathan Brown, offered himself this task of what was at that moment thought to be an attempt at mapping at an international thoroughfare over the Assam frontier. Another missionary, Oliver T. Outter, a printer, accompanied Brown for working for a small printing press, which major Tenkins advised to be taken as very necessary equipment (Baruah 1956).

It was really surprising to learn the activities of these Baptists in Assam how they mixed with the Assamese people and learnt their language partially in a short period, how they innovated a new literature and journalism and imparted a new education in a modern form of that language. How they fought in comradeship with a young Assamese civil officer, Anandayan Dhekijul Phukan. It is an interesting point to note that the Christian missionaries who even at the risk of their lives tried to spread Christianity in the state are remembered not for their activities towards the growth and development of modern Assamese language and literature (Barpujari 1977).

The history of press in Assam forms a fascinating study. The first printing press in Assam was brought by an American Baptist Missionary in Sibsagar in 1836 AD He published a series of brochures informing the public about the merits of Christianity and glorifying the biblical stories (Murthy 1966). The motto behind this was to propagate Christian religion. The first Assamese periodical 'Arunodaya' made its appearance in 1846 AD. Its first editor was an American missionary, Oliver T. Cutter. This journal has played a memorable part in shaping modern Assamese literature. The journal was regularly published for over 36 years (Baruah 1956).

The 'Assam Mihir' is considered the first known weekly newspaper in Assamese language. It made its appearance in1872.The first daily newspaper of Assam was "Batori". It was founded as a weekly in 1929. In 1935, it became a daily and came to be known as 'Dainik Batori'.

During 1935-1940, many weekly newspapers appeared in Assam. They were short-lived but have played their respective part in the progress of Assamese journalism. The Danik Assamiya that started in 1946 was the second daily newspaper of Assamese. Many newspapers in Assamese language were published but they have all ceased to appear. Journalism in

Assamese language has not developed for want of literacy and financial support. But now Assamese people have begun to take great interest in their language. More and more Assamese people are now feeling the importance of newspaper in Assamese language. At present many newspapers and periodicals are published from Assam in different languages. Among the English daily newspapers "The Assam Tribune", "The Sentinel" and "The North East Times" are popular. Among the Assamese dailies "Dainik Asom", "Aagir Batori", "Danik Janmavumi" "Aji", "Ajir Ahom", "Amar Ahom", "Assamiya Khabar", "Assamiya Pratidin" and "Danik Agradot" are popular.

There are also some Bengali dailies published from Assam. These are "Dainik Jugasankha", "Dainik Sonar Cachar", "Samayik Prasanga", "Silchar Times" and "Gati". "Purbanchal Prahari" and "Sentinal" are the Hindi newspapers published from Assam.

On December 1845, a general conference, which was held at Sibsagar under the guidance of Baptist Missionaries, had decided to bring out and 'Orunodoi Sambad Patra' This effort little continued up to Dec. 1850; then it was changed to Oruvodoi (strictly spelt as Orunodoi). Price was one rupee per annum in advance, or one and a half at the end of the year (Neog 1998)

The Orunodai was published in two sections—the magazine and the newspaper and the varying sizes of the two were maintained up to 1850. In that period the size of the Orunodai was eight pages. From 1851 the newspapers size was doubled to sixteen pages. The number of the readership of the Orunodai proves that it became popular among the educated people, both Christian and non-Christian. In the beginning in 1846, 249 Assamese persons subscribed the papers. The total number of subscribers came down to 440. In 1867-65, the number of subscribers went up to about 700. But after that period the numbers of subscribers are not available (Chakraborty 1979).

In the year 1871, the owner of the 'Auniati' Publication, Sri Duttadeb Goswami Prabhu, brought 'Dharmaprakash Tantra' from Calcutta for printing purposes, which was the second printing machine. In 1871, 'Assam Bilashini', the second newspaper of Assam came out.

In 1872, the first weekly newspaper, the 'Assam Mihir' was published by the Chidananda Press from Guwahati. But it lasted for a short time due to lack of sufficient support In 1873,it stopped appearing forever. An English section was also introduced in the'Assam Mihir' towards the closing date of it. It may be noted that the 'Chandrodaya' of the 'Dehing Tantra' was printed at Gauhati from the same Chidananda Press from which the 'Assam Mihir' had been brought out. It also could not be ascertained whether language of the paper was Assamese or Bengali (Neogi 1962).

The 'Assam Darpan' was published as a monthly magazine from Tezpur in 1873-74. But it could not take notable footsteps. Lakshinikant Barkakanti was the editor of this magazine. In that period, two other magazines were also published from Nowgaons. These two magazine focus towards the development of science, literature and religion (Bhagabati 2005).

The contribution of Assam did not stop with the closure of the Bialashini. In 1876 another paper under the title'Assam Dipak' was the first magazine published from the 'Dharma Prakash Tantra' from Guwahati. This paper lived just for one year (Baruah 1999).

Between the years 1871, the year of publication of the Assam Bilashini and 1876 of the publication as well as the closure of the Assam Dipak at least light magazines and newspapers were published in Assam. These years saw the beginning of a new era of Assamese literature and the activities of Hemchandra Goswami. But all of these magazines and newspapers did not exist longer. (Baruah 1999).

In 1882, the editor Hemchandra Baruah, brought out a bi-lingual weekly newspaper. But from July 1885 this newspaper came out as a daily.This time its subscribers were about 900. Abha Sankar Guha was the assistant editor (Neog 1998).

But out of these above cited magazines and newspaper only a few, viz. the Orunodoi, Assam Bilashini and Assam News played important and significant roler within their own orbits for promoting the growth of a modern intellectual background in Assam.

Role of the Press in the Pre-Independence Period

Though the paper 'Orunodoi' was primarily intended to spread the message of Christ, it did not remain a medium for sheer religious propaganda. In its contents it was western in character but it also contained translation of the Buranjis, articles on the evils of opium consumption, national history and regular feature on the tribals of the North-East like the Aka, the Abor (Adi), the Khamti, etc. Awaking the Assamese nationalism was an important contents in that period. Besides international and national news,the Orunodoi published purely local news also. In fact Nothan Brown used the paper as a vehicle of social reform. Brown was not only the founder editor he nursed this paper at every stage. Even then he sold the paper in the streets and markets of Sibsagar and others (Baruah 1956).

Various sorts of news and accounts of events took place in the Orunodoi. Some of them are the news of the death of a woman falling victim to a crocodile in the Dikhon (March1846) damage done by the flood, storm, fire, earthquake at Assam (July 1846) theft in the store room of the king Purandar Singha (August 1846), admission of Assamese students in the Calcutta Medical College, establishment of a market by Moniram Dewan at Arjunguri, a few buffaloes thundered to death at Kowerpur Mouza and so many news of such assorted nature were published in the Orunodei regularly. The content of the Orunodoi was both religious and secular in character (Neog 1998).

The publication of the Orunodoi, the first news magazine in Assamese in 1846 by the missionaries was a turning point in the history of modern Assamese language, besides widening the mental horizon of the Assamese people to the extent of bringing the world at large within their reach.

The 'Assam Bilashini' continued religious themes for twelve years, i.e., from 1871 to 1882. This paper not only focused 'Baishanab religion' but also on various sorts of international and national news and wrote uncountable articles and features.

Famous Assamese poetry-cum-drama literateur, Bholanath Das (1858-1929), serialized his Sitaharan Kavya in the Assam Bilashini from 1871. At the first instance of its appearance in 'Assam Bilashini' Bholanath Das had to face criticism for the Anglo-Bengali tone in his writing and for the curious verse form which was not known earlier in Assam (Das 1998).

Regarding the 'Assam News', Hemchandra Barua mentions the name of Iswarchandra Vidhya Sagar with respect in his autobiographical sketch in connection with his discussion about widow marriage. In his article 'Anik Biya Karoa Ajungur' and in his book notes on marriage systems of the people of Assam, he referred the system of polygamy and supported the cause of widow remarriage. In the 'Assam News' edited by him, he focused this view for creating a public opinion in favour of it. Though an editor was not a Brahmon himself, yet this attitude towards the traditional religious superstitions indicates a powerful influence of the Brahmo ideal on him. He also focused in his journal, on social justice to women, especially on casteism and illiteracy in the society. Moreover, Hemchandra tried to focus on the several problems of Assam and the Assamese language and nationality. Hem Chandra Barua, a towering personality of his age, was the harbinger of mode in Assam. An ardent reformer as he was Hem Chandra gave new directions to Assamese language, literature and its society (Das 1998).

The Post-independence Assamese Journalism

The post-Independence was a transition period in Assam, which transformed the mediaeval Assamese society to a modern one. Alike in other parts of India, introduction of social reforms, removal of social abuses and formation of modern provincial literature and development of the language are the major factors that helped in bringing about changes in the outlook of the Assamese people (Baruah 1999).

Already the need of a broad based provincial social organization was felt in the elite section with their background of western education. This section wanted to uphold the cause of the Assamese people. It has been observed that as the freedom movement in the country entered different phases, the relations between government and the press also changed rapidly.

The people of the North-Eastern India were habituated to an exclusive life without much contact with outside world. But with the beginning of the British rule the people had to give up their old habits and started to adopt a new outlook towards life. Naturally, its impact fell on the economic structure and with the expansion of the western education. A mini-commercial and industrial revolution had started in the region. Side by side, with this a number of Assamese journals were published with special reference to trade and commerce. In this context it should be noted that in the western world the newspaper first appeared in the form of a trade bulletin and later on it was transformed into a newspaper Assam Sahitya Sabha, the leading literacy organization of Assam, had played an important role in the life of the Assamese people since 1917. The eighth annual session was held in 1925 in which it decided to publish a quarterly organ of this literary organization. Accordingly, in October 1926 the Assam Sahitya Sabha Patrika appeared under the editorship of Chandarhar Baruah (1874-1961), a leading Assamese poet of that time. It also covered other relevant subjects like history, culture and economic condition of the state. It may be treated as research journal and continuing as such at present (Baruah 1964)

The history of the printing press in Assam is only ten years older than the history of Assamese journalism. The American Baptist Missionaries of Sibsagar was the centre for the Assamese printed work for long. In spite of the establishment of several printing presses from the beginning of the seventies the recorded number of the printed published work in Assamese was no encouraging. So, the need for newspapers and magazines were indispensable for creation of new readers and writers in the province (Borpuzari 1977)

The Bengali language and culture played a dominant role in the affairs of Assam for a good part of the nineteenth century. As a result of early contact with the company's rule the people of Bengal had the advantage of coming under the influence of English education and western liberal thoughts and ideas. The Indian press by and large was the product of the British rule and appeared first in the form of the Bengal press. Obviously, enlightened section of the Assamese opted for taking advantages from the Bengal press. Later on, indigenous efforts received a great fillip when Assamese was restored to its rightful place.

Large number of newspapers appeared from the Surma Valley, mostly in Bengali languages. It successfully tried to compete with the Bengali papers published outside the state. Sometimes, in rare occasions, a handful of papers also made an endeavour to publish an additional edition in Assamese for the benefit of other parts of the state. 'Saptahik Surma' was a Bengali weekly, which simultaneously published an Assamese edition of the paper. It appeared in 1943 under the editorship of Ramesh Ch. Das. It was printed and published from the Islamic Press of Sylhet. The paper mostly carried news on the Second World War. It seemed the paper was pro-government in character and was published with an intention to make the war effort popular among the people support the cause of the British government (Baruah 1999).

In sum, the press in Assam, like the Indian Press, has the original roots in the missionary efforts. Through the sources of origin in both the cases are extraneous, the press in India was initiated by the missionaries and was brought up systematically by the British for their administrative needs where as in Assam the press emerged and developed through the Assamese language and literature. In the course of the time the Assamese press took off and gained a self –reliant status. Administrative machinery came up to use it at a later stage. Today, the Assamese press has got a status which is well recognized in India.

REFERENCES

Barua B. K 1964 *History of Assamese Literature*, New Delhi:Sahitaya Acedami,

Baruah, Sunil Pawan 1956 *History of Journalism in Assam*, Morioni, Assam: Banti Sahitya Mandir.

Baruah, Sunil Pawan 1999 *Press in Assam:Origin and Development*, Guwahati : Lawyer's Book Stall.

Bhagabati, Radhika Mohan 2005 *Sambad Sambadpatra Aru Sambadikata*, Guwahati: Publication Board of Assam.

Borpujari H.K. (ed) 1977 *Political History of Assam 1826-1919*, Dispur: Government of Assam,

Chakraborty A, 1978 *History of Education of Assam*,Guwahati: Gauhati University.

Choudhury, Loho Biplap 1998 *NE Press fails to rise to occasion, Communicator:* April-June.

Das, Jogesh 1998 *'Orunodoi Bhasar Prati Hemachanda Baruah Patyakhyan : Assam News Abadan' in Saikia, Chandra Prakash(ed) Asamar Batri Kakat- Alochnir DersaBachariya Itihas*, Tribune Press Guwahati.

Nag, Amit Kumar 1998 *Asamat Prakasito Bangla Bhasar BatarikakatArihona Aru Krititya in Saikia,Chandra Prakash (ed) Asamar Batri Kakat-Alochnir Dersa Bachariya Itihas*, Tribune Press, Guwahati.

Neog Maheswar 1998 *'Orunodoi' in Saikia, Chandra Prakash(ed) Asamar Batri Kakat- Alochnir Dersa Bachariya Itihas*,Tribune Press Guwahati.

Neogi, Gautam 1977 *Role of Press in India's Struggle for Independence*: *Historical Judgment,* Indian Journalists Association, Platinum Jubilee Commemoration Volume.

6

The Barak Valley Press in the British Period

Alike other part of India, the wheel of journalism started moving in the Barak Valley since the last part of nineteenth century. The prime language of the valley is Bengali. So the newspapers being published from here are mostly in Bengali. Till today, Bengali is the key language of the valley's journalism, although some newspapers have been brought out in other Indian languages, viz., Manipuri, Dimasa, Hindi and English.

Origin

Origin of journalism in the valley is quite different from the rest of the country, due to topographical and political factors. The undivided valley in the pre-Independence era was known as 'Surma Valley' covering Cachar and Sylhet districts. The commencement of journalism was from 'Surma Valley'. Discussion on the origin of journalism in Barak Valley is never complete without reference to 'Surma Valley'. Sylhet was the heart of Surma Valley. Administration was directed from Sylhet. Sylhet had its own distinct place for creativity, literature and business. It was also the birth place of some great sons of the soil, who contributed the freedom movement and the field of journalism. Undeniably, it was the place of newspapers and, indeed, the first vernacular newspapers of Surma Valley saw the light of the day from Sylhet. In January 1875 "SRIHATTA PRAKASH" made its appearance under the editorship of Payeri Charan Das. Keeping consistency with the vernacular press started in Calcutta, the journalism in Surma Valley began with the sole aim to free India from the shackles of colonialism and to reform the Indian society. Due to lack of printing press, 'Srihatta Prakash' was printed from Calcutta. The great freedom fighter Bipin Chandra Paul edited 'PARIDARSHAK' which was first newspaper printed from Sylhet. Paridarshak had attained a distinguished place among the newspapers of Surma Valley for its noble mission. Sylhet was the place of pioneering journalism in Suma Valley, from the scattered throughout the valley and in Silchar too (Bhattacharjee 1942).

Silchar

Journalism started in Barak Valley as a part of the Surma Valley after the establishment of printing press at Silchar. The growth of printing press facilitated the progress of journalism in this valley. Babu Harekrishna Gupta was the pioneer to present the first printing press, 'SILCHAR PRESS' to the people of this sub-region in 1885. The first newspaper of the Barak Valley was a Bengali weekly, - 'SILCHAR' printed at Silchar press in 1889. "SILCHAR" considered as the earliest known newspaper was edited by Babu Bidhu Bhusan Sen who was a teacher of the Narshing Middle English School. Its publication was initiated by Mahesh Chandra Dutta and Anand Mohan Gupta. There has been a controversy related to the first publication date of the earliest newspaper, 'SILCHAR' among the researchers and journalists working in the field. But the reliable evidences have not yet been produced (Siru 1992)

The editor Babu Bidhu Sen was popularly known as Bidhu Pandit had a very powerful pen. He used it unsparingly against both officials and non-officials. His writing was full of satire and wit. So fearless was he that though serving in a school aided by the Government, he did not hesitate to attack the

Inspector of Schools and the D.P.I. Enraged by his satires, Wilson, the D.P.I., on one occasion, threatened to withdraw the grant from the school if the Pandit continued to be the editor of 'The Silchar'. As a result, the paper was discontinued for some years, but it was revived in 1897 when Wilson was no longer in the office. The editor soon resumed his fiery columns and carried on attacks on the district authorities and the Head Master of the Government High School. The Head Master sought permission of the D.P.I. to prosecute the editor for defamation while the Deputy Commissioner refused to recommend the exchange of the Assam Gazette with this paper. Bidhu Babu was a conservative caste Hindu and this conservatism brought him into tussle with the head master. The cook in the Hindu Hostel of the Government High School was a non-Brahmin and 'Silchar' raised the demand for a Brahmin cook. In its issue of 29th July 1903, the paper said:

> "Great inconvenience is felt by the students of the school for want of a Brahmin cook. The head master does not like to take any step in this connection because he is neither a Brahmin nor a Kayastha. We request the DPI to remove the inconvenience."

This episode reflects the contemporary social scene in Cachar. Untouchability was the definitely practiced. Even Bidhu Bhusan, though not a Brahmin himself, was serious for a Brahmin cook in students' hostel. Incidentally, the head master was Babu Abhaya Charan Das and for the charge of the editor he did not take any step. As a matter of fact, the head master for a long time had been pressing the authorities for a Brahmin cook. Although Bidhu Bhusan was censored for 'scurrilous writings', it may said that the Government High School was the actual target of his attack and not the head master.[1]

Bidhu Bhusan was the product of his own age and what appeared in the columns of his paper might not necessarily be his own views. As a journalist, he might have represented the contemporary public opinion. Nevertheless, Bidhur Bhusan Sen was the pioneer of journalism in Cachar. 'Silchar' was the only newspaper in the district in the last century and it played a commendable role in guiding public opinion and focusing attention on social and political problems.

In 1911 'Surma', another Bengali weekly, began its publication from the Aryan press which played very important role in freedom movement. The first editor was Pandit Chandraday Vidyavinode and was succeeded by Pandit Bhuban Mohan Bidyarnarva. The Aryan Trading Co. at Silchar was the owner and publisher. The paper was converted into a daily in 1914 and kept the people informed of the developments of World War I and other events too. Being discontinued for some years in the, twenties, the 'Surma' resumed its publication in the thirties under the editorship of Babu Nagendra Shyam - the eminent lawyer-literature of Cachar. In the forties the paper was edited by Hurmat Ali Barlaskar. Later he edited another Bengali weekly 'Azad'. Daring in spirit and constructive in criticism, the 'Surma' played a great role in guiding the public opinion in Cachar and sometimes forced the Government to note its views. It also acted as a fillip to the literary pursuits in Cachar by opening columns for young talents. Nagendra Chandra Shyam, Ashok Bijoy Raha, Ramendra Deshmukhya and Sudhir Sen were among the regular contributors.[2]

Like Bidhu Bhusan Sen, Pandit Bhuban Mohan Bidyanarva is a great name in the history of journalism of the valley. Besides his association with 'Surma', he edited 'Janasakti' and 'Deshbarta' from Sylhet. Earlier, he was associated with 'Hitavadi' and 'Sadhana' published from Calcutta and Dacca respectively. Bhuban Mohan was an ardent nationalist belonging to no political party and wielded his pen forcefully for the nation's cause. As a journalist he preached the swadeshi spirit and enthused the young men with the culture and heritage of India. He became the editor of Surma in 1912 and continued to edit it when it was converted into a daily in 1974. Bhunban Mohan had thus the unique distinction of editing the first daily newspaper published from Cachar. He was the editor of 'Samay' published from Silchar at that time (Das 1998).

Babu Bhuban Mohan Bidyarnaba was also the editor of 'Brahman Parishad Patrika', a quarterly Bengali journal of Brahmanical philosophy. It was the organ of the 'Silchar Brahman Parishad' and was first published on 24th April 1929. Printed by Babu Radhakanta Sadhya at the Sandhya press. The Brahman Parishad Patrika was published by Pandit Kalijay Nayapanchanan of Silchar. The object of the journal as stated in the declaration before the court was the social reform of Brahman society. The contents of the Patrika were always full of history of Brahmins and their activities and the most important thing is that they opposed the Harijan movement by Gandhiji through their Patrika. It is interesting to note here that the spirit for reform of Brahmin society in and around Silchar led to the formation of an organisation to reform the society, besides self criticism and reform stories. The patrika had worked for the society and Babu Bhuban Mohan and his colleagues had responded to the needs of time. The Patrika could not continue after the first three issues.[3]

'Bhabishyat', a Bengali monthly, made its appearance in 1926. It was edited by critic and lawyer Nogendra Chjandra Shyam of Shillongpatty, Silchar, and printed at the Calcutta Printing Works, Calcutta, and published from Ukilpatty Silchar. Notwithstanding so many hindrances, it continued its publication from Ukilpatty, Silchar, for a few years.

At that time another monthly came into being and continued for a period of two years. 'Navoyug' was published from Silchar in April, 1920 under the editorship of Mohendra Nath Choudhury but discontinued after two years. 'Shiksha Sevak', a literary quarterly, was published from Silchar in July 1925.[4]

In the third fourth decade of twentieth century a large number of periodicals and literary magazines were published In 1930 'Bartaman', a Bengali weekly started publication from Silchar. Its editor was Bhupendra Kumar Shyam. But 'Bartaman' could not last for a long time, discontinued just after three months of its publication. At that time the Guru

Charan College Majlis brought its handwritten magazine, 'Kundakali', in 1935 and the poet Rabindra Nath Tagore sent his blessings for its success. The college magazine, 'Purbasree', began to be published from 1940. 'Krishak', a monthly newspaper covering agriculture and agriculturists came out in July 1937. Its editor was Hurmat Ali Barlaskar but it could not impress the farmers and ceased the publication after two issues. 'Chamak', another fortnightly magazine, came out in 1939; its editor was Bhupendra Chandra Shyam. It could bring out nine issues only. Literary magazine, 'Suredoh', was brought out by Girija Nath Choudhury in 1938. It was a magazine of both in English and Bengali language.

'Manipuri' a monthly newspaper in Manipur language, came out at that time. It was published from Silchar in 1939 and the editor was Samarjit Singh (B.Sc., B.L). Later on it started its publication in Bengali also. It continued for a long time.

'Saptak', a weekly newspaper which contributed to the freedom movement in Barak Valley, was published in 1937. It was published from Silchar every Wednesday and printed at Jayanti Press. Kushi Mohan Das was its editor who was succeeded by Gajendra Chanda Dutta after some issues. In these publications, the initiative was taken by the Principal, A.K. Chanda of Law College and Tagore, blessed them all.

In 1940, the first newspaper edited by a woman came into publication., 'Vijoyini' as the organ of Silchar Mohila Samiti. Its editor was the first woman graduate of Cachar, Jotshan Chanda, wife of eminent educationist and leader A.K. Chanda. Later on she became the Member of Parliament. Another literary magazine 'Diganta' came out in 1940 edited by Parimal Purkayastha. It continued with a few issues only. [5]

The organ of nationalist 'Prachyabartya' weekly made its appearance in 1940, edited by Haresh Ranjan Bhattacharjee. It existed for 3 to 4 months. Edited by Monomohan Mazumdar and Kadarnath Choudhury, the mouth piece of Assam Education Department, 'Janashiksha' was published from Silchar in 1941.

Karimganj

Among the periodicals of the Barak Valley in the pre-Independence period Karimganj also contributed some weeklies and fortnightlies which also played great role in the freedom struggle. 'Panchajanya' and 'Muktinayak' were two noteworthy names. The former was a weekly and latter, a fortnightly. Another weekly newspaper 'Jagaran' was published from Karimganj with its stress on democratic socialism (Bhattacharjee 1993).

The 'Eastern Chronicle' published from Karimganj played a notable role during the early days of freedom movement in the valley. Bipin Chandra Paul, a patriot close to the region, was sentenced to six months imprisonment and sent to Boxer Jail in October 1907. He was released on 9th March 1908. The Eastern Chronicle reacting its own way welcomed his release. Referring to the then crisis in the Indian National Congress, the paper wrote that:

> "The citadel is yet to adverse reconciliation and a constitution for the Congress is being hatched in secret. The expectant eye of our people is not upon the coming heir who is to guide us to our destination".

Its writing was fearless by which it could mould and guide the public opinion. The 'Surma Valley Magazine', an English monthly, edited by Rev. W.H.S. Wood was published from Silchar in March 1927. It carried out the literary works. At that time the Tea Board of India brought out a magazine for the tea planters printed at Calcutta. It is interesting to note here that although printed at Calcutta, its cover page published from Silchar Assam.

Mojtilal Jagirdar took over the newspaper in latter part. It was banned in 1948. 'Samabay', mainly contributing to co-operative movement, was started as bi-fortnightly in 1939. Brojendra Kumar Aditya was its editor. It was published from Karimganj.

The first newspaper of Karimganj made its appearance during the British period. The credit for publishing first printed newspaper goes to Kailash Chandra Biswas. He had the distinction of launching 'Sreehatta Surida', a monthly newspaper from Karimganj, in April 1890. Before that some handwritten newspapers were making rounds. But with the publication of 'Sreehatta Surida', the real journalism began. Though the growth of journalism in Karimganj was mainly associated with 'Sreehatta Suridha' (1890) and 'Pravat' (1908) yet their impact was not very effective. The former one was mainly a religious paper and the latter a carrier of reformation campaign. The history of freedom struggle was also found in the pages of 'Pravat'. 'Sreebhumi', another monthly, was published in April 1915. It was edited by Satish Ch. Dev. 'Panchajanaya', a monthly, published in April 1930, was the first political newspaper of Assam. Its editor was Subodh Kumar Roy. It was the mouthpiece of 'Bharatiya Juba Andolan' and helped a lot to raise political consciousness among the people. The most remarkable development of journalism of Karimganj during the pre-Independence era was the publication of 'Pallibani' on May 1936. Its editor was Subodh Kumar Roy. For five years, this fortnightly was published from Karimganj. Later, it shifted to Habijganj (now in Bangladesh). 'Mukti Nayak', another fortnightly started in 1937. Its editor was Akhil Bandhu Chakraborty (Bhattacharjee 1942).

Hailakandi

Before Independence, some other newspapers also started publication from Silchar and Karimganj. But Hailakandi had no contribution in this regard during the era. 'Adhikar' the leftist organ, appeared in 1943. It was a bi-weekly edited by Achinta Bhatt and Anil Biswas.

Since 1889 the development of journalism in Barak Valley has been blended with unique mission freedom. Contribution of journalism was very important. On the one hand, it provided impetus to prose style and, on the other hand, moulded the public opinion in favour of freedom movement. The most beneficial job they did to carry out the spirit of nationalism and sense of oneness among the people of this sub-region. The newspapers also initiated social reform movement and inspired the people to shed off superstitions. But the newspapers of Barak Valley could not impress upon the people deeply, except the two eminent newspapers 'Silchar' and 'Surma'. Although the newspapers of this valley had served the people but the newspaper published from Sylhet dominated among the people and the market of Barak Valley. Average number of readers preferred to read these newspapers and some Calcutta based Bengali dailies. Those newspapers also gave priority to this region and carried out on the spot coverage of the event of this valley. So, it wasn't convenient to impinge upon the readers' psychology and hold the market for the newspapers of this valley. Moreover, Barak Valley had no proper infrastructure for newspaper publications in the pre-Independence period. Due to financial instability as well, so many publications could not last long. But the 'Silchar' in the early stage and 'Surma' and 'Arunodaya' in the later part were the exception. The contributions made by these newspapers to the Independence and development of the society were immense. Thus, in the pre-Independence era of the country, the valley contributed so many aggressive newspapers which carried forward the freedom movement.

In sum, the press in the valley emerged and grew in the environment and consciousness of the Indian freedom movement among the intellectuals. Local problems were consciously brought to the notice of the administration and the masses through the press. Looking to the region situated far away from the mainland, it generated a good number of publications. The valley press has an indigenous source of motivational source in the sense that the journalists and intellectuals were mostly the Bengali and were inspired by the activities of the press in the mainland of Bengal surrounding Kolkata and Dhaka. No doubt, the social, political and administrative climate was not much conducive for the development of the press but the nationalist zeal and cultural enthusiasm constantly inspired the intellectuals to continue the spirit of journalism. On Independence of India the press took breath in an environment of freedom and progress and this infused in the press a strong bout of spirit for nation building. The press started to take strides towards its professionalism and expansion among the masses.

NOTES

1. Amit Kumar Nag, a veteran journalist, Silchar was interviewed on 15th May 2004 at Club Road, Silchar.
2. Monojendra Shyme, a veteran journalist, Silchar, was interviewed on 22nd Sept. 2004 at Ukilpatty, Silchar.
3. Atin Das, a veteran journalist and Ex Editor of Jugashankha, Silchar, was interviewed on 30th Sept. 2004 at Rongpur, Silchar.
4. Monojendra Shyme, a veteran journalist, Silchar, was interviewed on 22nd Sept. 2004 at Ukilpatty, Silchar.
5. Amit Kumar Nag, a veteran journalist, Silchar was interviewed on 15th May 2004 at Club Road, Silchar.

REFERENCES

Bhattacharjee, Bijit Kumar 2000 *Atandra O Barak Upatakaya* Bangla Kayaba Charcha, Hailakandi: Sihatiya Prakashan

Bhattacharjee, Bijit Kumar 2002 *Uttar Purva Bharater Bangla Sahitiya,* Hailakandi: Sihatiya Prakashan

Bhattacharjee, Jatin Mohan 1942 *Srihattabashi Sampadiya Abong,* Srihatta O Cachar Haite Prakashito Sambad Patrika, Syleth: Bangladesh

Bhattacharjee, Usharanjan 1993 *Srihatta Sahitya Parishat O Patrika,* Calcutta: Oriental Publishers.

Das, Atin 1998 *Satabdir Taithya Punji, Barak Upatakaya Banga Sahitya Sambelan,* Silchar: Prasongik Printers and Publication.

Das, Kaliprasana 1964 *Sambadpatra Sebay Srihatter Sthan*, Shillong.

Nag, Amit Kumar 2000 *Assmer Batri Kakat, Abcanir Dersa Barchariya Itihass*, Tribune Press, Guwahati

Mahiudin, Siru 1992 *Sylether Satabarsher Sambad Patra,* Syleth: Bangladesh, Akkhar Computer.

7

The Barak Valley Press in the Post-independence Period

After Independence in 1947 the mission of journalism became a profession. Young journalists took it as profession, new trends were set up and some other developments occurred in the post-Independence era. The journalism totally changed during the period. Newspaper publication got momentum in the period and the number of publications increased enormously. Revolutionary off-set machine was set up and used for newspaper publication. Eminent dailies appeared. In fact, Indian journalism moved forward in the valley with new and new improved technologies,. After 1947 many periodicals and dailies made their appearance and journalism spread through out the valley. Karimganj and Hailakandi also contributed the newspapers of substance

When the partition took place, intellectuals, along with others came to India. Some eminent journalists of Sylhet also came to India with their press and publication. They resumed their publication of newspapers after settling in the Barak Valley. 'Janasakti' and Jugashakti' were also among them. Both the newspapers were of repute in Sylhet. After partition they travelled to Barak Valley in India (Bhattacharjee 1942).

Newspapers from Silchar

In the history of the Barak Valley journalism, Silchar has always held distinct place. Before and after Independence, Silchar was leading in the newspaper publications in the valley. Silchar has the credit for the first daily newspaper of the valley. Till today, Silchar based daily newspapers dominate the valley. After 1947, Silchar contributed a lot of periodicals and daily newspapers with their noteworthy contribution.

Just after Independence, 'Janashakti' started its publication from Silchar. It was an influential newspaper of Sylhet. 'Janashakti' was started in 1921 and its founder editor was Bhuban Mohan Bidyarnav. Later, Nistaran Gupta took charge and shifted the newspaper to Silchar. After its publica-tion resumed from Silchar, 'Janashakti' could not continue long. Baidyanath Nath from Silchar started 'Muktipradip', a bi-weekly, in 1948. But in 1949, it stopped its publication. Then, in 1950, 'Arunodoya' – the renowned weekly of the valley made its appearance. It was started on 26th January 1950 edited by Sunil Kr. Dutta Roy. Chandan Sengupta took over the newspaper in 1991. It is continuing its publication from the Arunodaya Press Shillongpatty (now Ullaskar Dutta Sarani), Silchar. The contribution of Arunoday towards language movement of Barak valley was notable(Das 2002).

It was at that time that 'Prantojyoti', the first daily of the Barak Valley, came into existence. 'Prantojyoti' was first started, as bi-weekly, by the name of 'Jyoti' on 12 January 1956 from the Silchar Press. Its founder- editor is Jotindra Chandra Dutta. In 1964 it became daily and till today it is continuing its publication. But in, 1961-62, 'Prantojyoti' gave a new look to the daily newspaper to cope up with the situation. At that time the language movement of Barak Valley was going on. The *Satyagrahis* fought for their Bengali language and the Government tried to impose Assamese language forcefully in place of Bengali. The mother tongue, Bengali, is the language of the majority of the people of the valley. Night curfew was imposed in Silchar and the people were eager to know about the latest development of the movement. The editor then tried to bring out a daily newspaper to inform the people. At the time of language movement, 'Prantojyoti' was brought out in post card size. It contained just headlines. The people of Silchar waited in the morning for this daily 'telegram'. 'Prantojyoti' made remarkable achievements during the language movement. Jogendra Choudhury – founder principal of Cachar College later became the M.P. He addressed the parliament at that time, quoting 'Prantojyoti'. It was a notable achievement of 'Prantojyoti'[1].

In the first issue of 'Prantojyoti' the editorial criticized the doctors' attitude and the role of newspapers, because the editor's sister died of a disease at night. He himself contacted the doctors but all refused to come out and, without treatment she died. The editor even approached the newspapers to publish the event but none of them showed the courage to publish it. The proprietor editor, Dutta criticized the doctor in his first issue. The editorial impressed the people. The people of this valley still remember 'Prantojyoti' for its writings. At that time another weekly came out in Silchar, which later, became the leading daily of the valley.

It is 'Jugasankha', published first on 17th December 1950 from Silchar. It was a weekly, printed in letter press machine and crown size paper. The founder- editor was late Baidyanath Nath a teacher, who subsequently joined the freedom movement and started a newspaper entitled 'Muktipradip' in 1948. It was a Congress mouth piece. In 1970 on the death of founder editor his son, B.K. Nath, took over the charge during 1970s. It was the highest circulated weekly in the valley. In 1982 it was converted into a daily and associated with a group of talented youth writers like Atin Das, Anadi Chakraborty, Jishu Chanda and so on. In 1983 it was shifted to Guwahati where it was the first publication of a Bengali daily. 'Dainik Ahom', and 'Nutan Ahomia' were the twice a week periodicals. After 'Dainik Ahom' it was the second newspaper published in 4 to 6 pages on sheet page. It continued up to 1989. Then, its publication was suspended because a fire gutted the press and the building and machinery were destroyed. After the setback, it started printing on off-set press. Subsequently, it suspended its publication because of financial problems. On 9th May 1995 it resumed publication on off-set with computerized composing. Since then its circulation has been growing up[2].

'Gati' another bi-weekly was started in 1966. Its editor was Dipendra Das. In eighties, it became daily and Jotin Deb Roy took the editorship. It was published from the letter press and had a good circulation in the early eighties. Although it is published till the day, yet its circulation is limited. 'Barak', another bi-weekly started in 1966. Golam Osmani was its founder editor. Atin Das took the charge in 1933. It mainly contains political articles of different writers. 'Prantiya Samachar'; a weekly, edited by Horendra Chandra Sen was started in June 1964. It became bi-weekly on 2nd October 1990 and Ataur Rahman became the editor .[3]

'Ahuti', another bi-weekly, was published in August 1969. Chandan Sen Gupta was its editor. It was a Lenin-Mao ideology based newspaper. Its editor was arrested on 22 April 1907 and the publication was stopped. 'Sapath', a daily, brought out by Kamalendu Bhattacharjee and Atin Das jointly in 1970-72. But after sometime its publication ceased. In 1972 another monthly newspaper 'Pathsala' was published. It usually published the news items, which were concerned with the problems of primary teachers (Bhattacharjee 2002).

'Sonar Cachar' a notable name in the history of journalism of Barak Valley, made its appearance as a bi-weekly on May 1975 (25 Baishak 1382 B/s). Its editor was Ranobir Roy. The age of Sonar Cachar can be considered the golden age of the Barak journalism. Since early eighties it became daily. Earlier, it was printed in the letter press at Nibedita lane, Rangirkhari, which is now popularly called Sonar Cachar Gali. Then, it was shifted to Shyama Prasad Road, Silchar and started publication on off-set printing with computerized composing. Sonar Cachar is the first standard size newspaper of the valley, having good circulation. It is the first publication which adopted off-set press in newspaper publication in the valley. Few years later, it emerged the largest circulated newspaper in the North East. Sonar Cachar brings out the account of local events, regional events and to some extent national events also. It also contains articles on political and literary matters. Its articles were strict against the rampant corruption of government officials and political leaders. Some factual news were also given by some by some interested groups of people. They even attacked the press and reporters of Sonar Cachar and burnt down a huge number of copies of Sonar Cachar in different places. In spite of all these Sonar Cachar is combatting the corruption and malpractices and maintaining its popularity and progress.[4]

'Samayeek Uphar' was brought out by Swapan Dev from 5th March 1977. It is a weekly newspaper which continues its publication till today. "Samayeek Prasanga", another weekly, edited by Taimur Raja started in 1977-78. Later, it became bi-weekly. It is now a daily newspaper published on colour offset. 'Cachar Times' a Bengali weekly, was started on 12th September 1977 and continued up to 1987. Its first editor was Bhudev Bhattacharjee. Then, Deepan Dewanjee took the charge of editorship and turned it into Bengali bi-weekly. It is continuing till date.[5]

In the eighties, several periodicals came into existence. Some of them are continuing and some have stopped their publications. This period is considered the golden period of the newspapers in the valley. Sajal Kanti Biswas started 'Anchalik Barta' on 12th January 1981. 'Bartalipi' was started by Sanat Kairi in January 1985. It was a weekly newspaper. But now it is published by Prasongik Press with Partha Bhattacharjee as its present editor. Earlier, Sanat Kairi had another weekly, 'Abosan', which continued only for six months. 'Sonar Desh', a bi-lingual weekly, started its publication on 31st Dec. 1982. It was edited by Pran Gopal Roy. Later, on 4th July 1992, it became a bi-weekly. It is continuing its publication. 'Barak Darpan' a Bengali fortnightly, was started on 25th December 1989 and became weekly on 5th January 1990. It is edited by Babli Adhikari and published from Silchar.

'Silchar Times' another Bengali daily of this period, came into existence as a bi-fortnightly on 1st January 1991 and became daily on 14th April 1994. It is published in the letterpress at Hospital Road, Silchar. Its editor is Sanant Kairi. As it was a letterpress and hand composed newspaper it could not compete with other dailies. But now it has turned to offset press. 'Silchar Times' often carry out good writing with criticism of the working and policy of administration. Besides, 'Silchar Times' is always conscious to save the Indian culture. 'Silchar Times' protested the Beauty Competition that was held at Silchar in 1996. 'Turjya', a weekly, edited by Samir Dey, was started on 3rd January 1983. 'Maitrai Bani', a bi-weekly was started by Soraj Kumar Das on 16th December 1989. Then, Santosh Kumar Das took over it. 'Apanjan' appeared as monthly in 1989 and became daily in 1993 under the editorship of Pijush Kanti Das. 'Apanjan' continued till the mid of 94.[6]

Silchar has a distinction of being the place of publication of so many news papers and journalism. Apart from the aforesaid newspapers there are 'Anjana' (by Nazrul Islam), 'Amar Barak', 'Barak Darpan', and 'Matribhumi' etc., there are some fortnightlies namely, 'Barak', 'Pally Darpan' and Cachar Lipika'. One English daily 'The Frontier Sun', edited by Mridul Roy is also now getting the recognition. It was a publication of Sonar Cachar Group. 'Eastern Progress' and English Monthly edited by Pijyush Kanti Das, was started in December 1996. It was a progressive newspaper and deals with the problems of North-East, especially the Southern Assam. But after some issues it ceased the publication. Two energy related weekly newspapers of Silchar are also moving ahead. They are ' The Energy Era' and the 'Oil Fields Times'. The former is publication of Sonar Cachar Group, edited by Anita Roy till date, and the latter, a publication of Jugasankha Group. But now 'Oil Field Times' does not exist (Das 1998).

Newspapers from Hailakandi

If the newspapers' contribution in Hailakandi district is explored one finds no contribution at all before the

Independence. In 1947, the first newspaper, 'Janamat', was started by Dr. Amulya Ratan Sengupta. The freedom fighter Birendra Kr. Das, mainly contributed to the newspaper. A great influence occurred by his Article 'Pukur Churi'. It was related to the P.W.D. functioning. Against such writing, an engineer of that department filed a case in Shillong affecting its publication.

In 1950 another two weeklies the 'Nabayan' and the 'Cachar', were published. But after publication of some issues they were stopped. The first editor of the 'Cachar' was Santaram Shekhar Bhadra. After his resignation, Digendra Nath Kabirangan became the editor in-charge of the newspaper. After him Amulya Choudhury took the charge of editorship for some days it was continued by him. In the year 1972, the then M.L.A. Santosh Kumar Roy, took over its editorship. But he discontinued later on (Bhattacharjee 2002)

A weekly, 'Dhaleswari', edited by Nani Gopal Dey was started in 1967. Dey was a freedom fighter. In 1947 he became the student Congress General Secretary and he involved himself in the politics actively. He joined the Forward Block, then P.S.P, thereafter Janata Dal and discontinued the publication of 'Dhaleswari'. But recently this newspaper has been resumed from Silchar with assistance of Sankar Dey.

During 1950s, several newspapers were published but all of them have discontinued. 'Prantik' edited by Amulya Choudhury came out from the Bharati Press. Sudhir Dutta started the 'Udayan'. Later on, it was shifted to Dharmanagar which is now in Tripura. Shakti Dhar Choudhury started 'Swaraj'. Harendra Chandra Paul published a weekly, 'Janakalyan'. A weekly, 'Jagoroni', was started by Nripen Kr. Choudhury. Krishna Singha started the 'Ganadut'. In 1950s another two English weekly newspapers were published from Hailakandi Town; 'The Sentinel' and 'The Voice'. The Sentinal was started by Captain Subodh Dutta and "The Voice" by Amiya Kr. Nandi. The latter was continued for six months.

During the movement of "Bhasha Andolan", another newspaper 'Nabodhara' edited by Purna Chandra Purkayastha and Usha Ranjan Chandra, was started. In 1972-73 Hari Prasannya Sen edited and published newspaper "Gramya Jiban" with the assistance of Abdul Latif Laskar. In 1974-75, Hari Prassanya Sen started another newspaper "Grammya Adhikar". But after two years it was closed. But in 1980 it was revived. Nazmul Hussain Mazumdar and Matiur Rahman jointly started the newspaper with the name "Asanta". In 1969, "Purbayan' was published from Hailakandi under the editorship of famous writer Saktidhar Choudhury. It was a weekly paper. Now it is not regularly publishing[7].

Nazmul Hussain Mazumdar individually started a weekly newspaper - 'Uttar Parba'. In 1978 a weekly, "Banga Shree", was started. It was edited by Tayabur Rahman Mazumdar. Later on, "Banga Shree" was renamed to "Dalim" which is continuing for the last 17 years. At the close of 1980s, a weekly, 'Dibakar' from Lala, edited by Abdul Kalam Mazumdar was published. In 1981 Ujjal Kr. Deb started an English Weekly- "Cachar Tribune". It is a regularly published newspaper since its commencement. Now, it is the only English weekly from Hailakandi. During 1980s Jalanta Sengupta started another newspaper weekly - "Mahakal" which published interesting news. But after some months it was closed. "Bajra Kishan" - a weekly edited by Debashish Purkayastha was started. Only after two months it was closed.

In June 1993 "Bajra Kishan" was revived. Then Subhas Ch Roy edited it up to 1994 January. This newspaper started a new trend in journalism and influenced the readers to some extent. During 1980s "Gana Surya" was the newspaper edited by Chandan Ghosh. It exist no longer now. District Co-operative Society's newspaper, "Samabay Sambad". We was sometime published by the editor Santosh Kumar Roy. Recently, a Manipur weekly, "Barak Tompak" has been brought out by the editor was Phanindra Singha. Another weekly, "Barak Jyoti", has appeared from Panchgram. Editor of this newspaper is Abdus Sukkar Choudhury. During 1980s Biswajit Paul

Choudhury edited another newspaper "Milon" which ceased after some issues.

Newspapers from Karimganj

Though the entire pre-Independence period is the beginning of journalism in Karimganj, the post-independence period has witnessed the subsequent growth. During this period, people were coming forward to take journalism as profession. A new development was the growing of commercialization of the press. The importance was given to advertisements. It is seen that before the Independence the newspapers were not commercial but after the Independence emphasis on commercials increased because of the professional attitude.

"Jugashakti" is the first successful commercial weekly newspaper from Karimganj. It actually started on 6th December 1936 from Sylhet. Its editor was Bidhu Bhusan Choudhury. After the partition of India, it was shifted to Karimganj in 1947. It is the oldest newspaper of Karimganj, which is existing till today. After the death of Bidhu Bhusan Choudhury his son Samarjit Choudhury became the editor. Bidhu Bhusan Choudhury was an eminent journalist of this area. The paper is printed from Jugashakti Press, Karimganj. It is an urban based newspaper and its present circulation is nearly 3000. In 1981, it was started as "Dainik Jugashakti" from Silchar But unfortunately, due to various hindrances, this existed for a year only. The weekly "Jugashakti" has its readership in Shillong, Guwahati, Calcutta and some parts of the N.C. Hills.[8]

"Ganabani" was the second weekly paper published from Karimganj in 1948. Its editor was J. L. Goswami. It was printed from the Sree Press, Karimganj. Though "Ganabani" reflected ability, yet its publication was stopped in 1952 because of various difficulties.

"Jagaran", a weekly paper, started in 1956, was edited by Jatindra Ranjan Deb, Ramendra Nath Roy and Mohendra Bhusan Dutta. It was mainly a leftist (C.P.I.) organ. It is not continuing.

"Purbachal", another Bengali weekly, was published on 15th March 1950 under the editorship of Subodh Chandra Dhar. But it has ceased publication due to financial crisis.

"Chabuk", a monthly paper, appeared in 1958 its founder editor was Bomkesh Biswas. Nirmal Das, Jyotirmoy Choudhury and Pulen Das took the editorship later on. The paper was initiated by the student leader, Ranjan Das. The "Chabuk" protested against corruption and contemporary malpractices of local administration. It launched anti-corruption campaign through its writing against the Government officers, public administrators and society's influential persons.

"Karimganj" was the another weekly newspaper published from Karimganj Press in 1954. It was edited by Nabokumar Bhattacharjee.

"Nabojug" weekly was started by Ramesh Chandra Biawas on 7th May 1955. Its recent editor is Rahul Das and it is printed from Nabayug press. It is one of the oldest newspapers of Karimganj existing till today. It is an urban-based newspaper. Though it is continuing but not published regularly.

"Dristipath", a complete rural based weekly, appeared on April 1962. It is a bi-lingual (Bengali and Dimasa) newspaper published simultaneously from Karimganj and Halflong. Its Bengali section was edited by Bhupendra Kumar Singh and Dimasa section was edited by Benani Dampri and Joyraj Singh.

"Danka" edited by Kripeshn Chandra Bhattacharjee was started on 17th July 1972 as a bi-weekly. Probably it is the first bi-weekly newspaper of Karimganj. It became weekly in 1975. Kamdev Bhattacharjee took over the paper later on. It was an investigative newspaper from National Press.

"Kushiara" another weekly, appeared under the editorship of Ramkrishan Banik on 30th November 1976. The paper is continuing its publication from Paramananda Press, Karimganj.

"Tirtha Bhumi" started by Satu Ray on 8th April 1978. It has been printed from Ratan Printing Press. It is exting but is published irregularly.

"Nabobarta Prasanga" edited by Habibur Rahaman is a bi-weekly newspaper appeared in April 1986. It is published simultaneously from Karimganj and Diphu and printed at Modern Printer, Karimganj. It is the only newspaper of Karimganj, which circulated to Saudi Arabia.[9]

"Anandajyoti" is another weekly started in 1986 by G. L. Goswami. Later, G.R. Goswami took over the charge and is printed it at Jyoti Printers.

H.K. Roy started "Karimganj Sangbad" in 1993. It is a weekly newspaper printed from Radha Ramon Press.

"Challenger Barta" is the only English weekly of Karimganj, which was started on 28th February 1994 and edited by B.G. Bhattacharjee-a retired A.C.S. officer It is printed at Modern Press. Mainly it deals with the problems of the urban life.

"Gram Kushiara" edited by Protima Sharma appeared on October 1995. It is published from Barapunji of Karimganj and printed at the Jyoti Printers. In March 1996 the paper changed to "Saptahic Gram Chabi". Some other papers were published from Karimganj. But they could not continue their publications after a few issues. "Sangbad Davani", "Samayer Ahban", "Aganiban", "Mahanayak", "Sjingla Prabaha", and "Ghar Ghar" have stopped their publication.

"Kalikusum" a bi-lingual and bi-monthly magazine type newspaper started on September 1995. It is published in both Assamese and Bengali. Its editor is Atiqur Rahman Choudhury.

"Patha Nirdesh", the first sports and cultural magazine from Karimganj was published in 1950. It was printed from the Union Press. It was a quarterly edited by Nishith Ranjan Roy.

"Purbaprantik", a weekly was published from Karimjanj in the year 2001. But it had to cease its publication after some issues.

It has been found that all the newspapers published from Karimganj are either weekly, fortnightly or monthly. There is no daily. The most commend able development of the journalism in Karimganj is the starting of "Dainik Protibedan", a daily newspaper, started on 6th June 1996. It was edited by G. L. Goswami and printed at the Jyoti Printers. Unfortunately, the paper had to stop its publication just after three months.

"Dainik Protibadan" has had within a short life of its appearance many notable achievements in the development of journalism in Karimganj District. Its style and way of presentation was fascinating. But due to lack of modern technology offset printing and financial instability, it could not last long.

Magazine Journalism

Magazine Journalism is not a new concept in Barak Valley. It has been there since the pre-Independence era. But was not very strong. At present there is not found a very good number of magazines here. From the pre-Independence era, no magazine could sustain long period. Most of the magazines had more or less little character. Some of these stopped after sometime. A few of them were revived under the same or other editors.

Earlier, magazine journalism was considered to be the useful tool for increasing cultural awareness in the valley. That time small magazines played their role very well.

The standard of magazine journalism has also been upgraded in the course of time. New techniques and concepts are continuously being tried and used in the development process. Indeed it has come a long way from the old printing technique to the present day offset printing with coloured cover pages. Magazines on different topics and for different types of readers are being published from time to time.

About the beginning of magazine journalism in the Barak Valley, the picture is hazy and not very clear. According to most of the interviewed persons, 'Saptak', a weekly magazine, started in Silchar in 1937 is considered the first magazine in the valley.

Another small but important magazine of the pre-Independence era is 'Diganta'. It was started and edited by two eminent poets, Sudhir Sen and Ramendra Deshmukhya. After Independence, a good number of magazines were started from time to time. In 1950, 'Ahawan' was started by Bijoy Chowdhury. It believed in the ideology of Lord Rama i.e. equal justice for every segment of society and people. In 1960 'Ishara' another magazine by Gulam Kibria came out which lasted up to 1970. In 1965, 'Kartik' came out. 'Atandra' is a magazine with Saktipada Brahmachari and Bimal Chowdhury as the editors. It came out in the same year. 'Lubdhak' a magazine edited by Dinesh Lal Roy an 'Shatabdi' by Atin Das came out in 1966. In 1969 'Shapath;' and anti-rivalry magazine to 'Atandra' came out with Kamalendu Bhattacharjee as its editor. 'Satakratu', a story based magazine with Tapodhir Bhattacharjee and Nikhilesh Bhattachajee as editors, came out in 1970. During 1970s and 1980s there were some magazines in the region but detailed information is not available. Still, in 1979, 'Ityadi' with Sujit Das as editor came to limelight. In 1980 'Amader Samakal', a revolutionary magazine with Hitendra Bhattacharjee and Sanjib Kr. Das as its editors, started its publication. It is a revolutionary magazine with new concepts in comparison to its contemporary magazines. In 1985, 'Pratisrot' a magazine with Partha Pratim Mitrta as editor was started. It had feature stories, short stories and poetry as its content.

In 1980-90, magazine journalism had many prominent ladies from this area as editors. 'Ma-Nishad', a cultural magazine had Chabi Gupta as its editor. 'Samachar' had Dipali Dutta Chouwdhury and 'Mukul', a children magazine with Deepali Choudhury as their editors. The magazines are still continuing. 'Chotoder Pata' another children's magazine with Dola Deb as its editor was also there in the field for sometime. In 1990 there came another magazine, 'Kha', with Soumitra Baishya as its editor, which is still very much present in the field. Other magazines like 'Akshar' is also published from Silchar but not very regularly. 'Kallipi', a news magazine edited by Sandip Acharya and Param Bhattacharya started in 1996. But it stopped publication after sometime. It is quite surprising to note that though the Bengali speaking community constitutes a major segment of the population in the north-east, there is almost not a single Bengali news magazine published regularly. 'Prasangik Kichhu Katha' was launched as a purely commercial news magazine with a view to cater to the demand of the Bengali speaking community of the region. It was also the first and only commercial offset printed magazine in Silchar. It started its publication from Guwahati as a small magazine in 1994. Then, it was not regular in its publication. The last circulation of this magazine was 3000 copies per issue. It had its market in Karimganj, Dharmanagar, Udharbond, Guwahati and Haflong along with Silchar. Another literary magazine, which started in November 1998, is 'Pandulipi' with Parthajit Bhattacharjee as its editor.[10]

Role of Press During Language Movement[11]

Role of Calcutta Newspaper

The Calcutta based newspapers like 'Amrita Bazaar Patrika', 'The Hindustan' (English), 'Jugantar' and 'Ananda Bazar Patrika' gave a little coverage of the movement For recognition of Bengali as the official language, eleven persons were shot dead, in front of the Railway station at Tarapur (Silchar) on 19th May 1961.

Silchar Publication

Barak valley journalism has also been performing its obligation to social upliftment since pre-Independence.

'Janasakti' was started in 1921 from Silchar, which played a vehement role to sensitize the society in the campaign. It was Niren Dey editor of Janasakti during the struggling period who wrote various articles against Bimola Prasad Chaliha Government in his editorial pulse. He strongly criticized against the Language Bill Act that was passed in the State assembly on 24th October 1960. The Act was to make Assamese an institutional lingua-franca. In 1961 the population of undivided Cachar was 13, 78,476. In 1950 another renowned weekly

'Arunodaya' paper of the Barak Valley made its appearance. Editor of this paper was Sunil Kumar Dutta Roy who also played an important role during the language movement

The 'Prantojyoti' the first daily of Barak Valley came into existence on 12th January 1956. It was a weekly published under the editorship of Niva Rani Dutta. During that time, the night curfew was imposed in Silchar and the people were anxious to know about the latest position of the movement. The editor brought out its daily sister newspaper like post card size issues named 'Telegram'. It contained only messages about the movement. 'Prantojoyti' made remarkable achievement in the time of language movement". Mr. Jogendra Choudhury founder principle of Cachar College who later became M.P. raised the matter in the parliament too.

In 17th December 1950, 'Jugasankha' was published from Silchar under the editorship of Baidyanath Nath. The editor and other journalist of Jugasankha had taken critical attitude while writing against the political parties which were not in support of the movement. This paper united all the people and made the youth aggressive to jump into the struggle (Paul Choudhury 2002).

Karimganj Publication

There were three weekly papers published from Karimganj at that time. They are 'Navoyug', edited by Ramesh Chandra Biswas, 'Jugashakti', edited by Bidhubushan Choudhury and Purbachal edited by subodh Ch. Dutta. 'Navoyug' was started on 7th May 1955, 'Jugashakti' was shifted to Karimganj in 1947 and 'Purbachal' was started in 1950. These three newspapers were involved in the language movement with various agenda. Scanned copies of these newspapers, one each, are shown here.

Hailakandi Publication [5]

During the movement of 'Bhasha Andolan', 'Navodhara' edited by Purna Chandra Purkayastha and Usha Ranjan Chandra Bhattacharjee played a significant role in this regard.

'Purbayan' edited Nitish Bhatacharjee also played an important role.

The martyrs are:

1. Sachindra Pal
2. Satyndra Dev.
3. Sunil Sarkar
4. Kamala Bhattacharjee
5. Kumud Ranjan Das
6. Toroni Devnath.
7. Kanilal Niyogi
8. Birendra Sutradar
9. Chandicharan Sutradar
10. Hitesh Biswas
11. Sukumol Purkayastha

Besides, hundreds of people were injured during the firing incident. The leaders who were actively involved were:

1. Artitosh Paul Choudhury (Silchar),
2. Alzdur Rohaman Choudhuyr (Hailakandi).
3. Nripoti Choudhury (Karimganj),
4. Keshab Chakrobarthy (Hailkandi),
5. Nalini Kanti Das (Silchar),
6. Prof.Sarath Nath (Silchar),
7. Bishyawath Upapadhya (Silchar),
8. Hurmot Ali Barlaskar (Silchar),
9. Mohitush Purkayastha (Silchar).

Some New Trends[12]

New Technology

The press in Barak Valley played a leading role in creating a political climate. The papers succeeds mainly because of their logical editorial policy and strict adherence to journalistic principles and techniques. The masthead contained a sentence which stressed the press. It also realized the importance of cartoons, now introduced in the all leading dailies of Barak Valley. The three leading dailies started publishing their copies in colour offset. They have satellite connection, too.

Contents

The press in Barak valley is not only concerned with the get-up of the paper but it is also equally concerned with its contents. Earlier, the contents were mostly on political issues but the trend has changed. The press in Barak Valley is now stressing development issues, too.

Anti Imperialism

In international sphere the press in Barak Valley supported national freedom movements everywhere. It condemned repression by the British in Iran and South Africa when the imperialism was in its heyday in Asia and North Africa. It also supported uprisings against Europeans in Morocco, Libya and Sudan.

Variety

Going through all leading papers of Barak Valley one finds a variety of topics discussed almost regularly in the paper. It should be kept in mind that most of the newspapers then confined themselves to articles and write-ups related with religion. The press in Barak valley took a different path. Besides discussing the topics of general issues, it published articles on science, e.g., micro-telescope, wireless telegraphy (teleprinter), sea mines, torpedo, desalination plant, levitated railway, theory of evolution, radium, geology and astronomy. It had also articles on archeology, especially on the new findings. There were also articles on the use of new technology in crimes, air war and use of dogs in the war.

Style

Almost all newspapers in the Barak Valley have basically a rhetoric style. The words were made to dance according to the editor's tunes and to a appropriate place. The same thing appeared with different ways of reasoning to make a point clear. The whole thing was summarized with an appropriate couplet or quadratic verse.

In sum, the Independence led to a flutter of many more publications of newspapers and magazines in the valley. From all the three towns the publications rolled out frequently along the circulation of the Calcutta based newspapers. Gradually, some of the locally emerging publications got established and they replaced the Calcutta based ones in many respects but not in totality. The diversity of population till date offers the conditions for survival of various publications- national, regional and local. Moreover, after Independence the press changed not only spirit and objective of the publication but also the contents and technology. The press gradually brought into its coverage various news, themes and sections of society. But the political news and themes dominated the press. Along with growing print technology and professionalism the journalism has been coming under the eclipse of yellow journalism.

NOTES

1. Jatindra Chandra Dutta, founder Editor of Dainik Prantojyoti, Silchar, was interviewed on 24nd Sept. 2004 at Prantojyoti Office, Silchar
2. Jatindra Chandra Dutta, founder Editor of Dainik Prantojyoti, Silchar, was interviewed on 24nd Sept. 2004 at Prantojyoti Office, Silchar

3. Atin Das, a veteran journalist and Ex Editor of Jugashankha, Silchar, was interviewed on 30th Sept. 2004 at Rongpur, Silchar
4. Paritosh Paul Choudhuty, a veteran journalist and an Activist of Language Movement Silchar, was interviewed on 26th June 2004 at Subhas Nagar, Silchar
5. Amit Kumar Nag, a veteran journalist, Silchar was interviewed on 15th May 2004 at Club Road, Silchar
6. Jyotilal Choudhury, a veteran journalist and Senior Correspondent of "The Sentinel", Silchar, interviewed on 5th June 2004 at Ahsram Road, Silchar
7. Nitish Bhattachajee, editor, Purbayan. Hailakandi, Assam was interviewed on 16th Jan 2005 at S.S. College, Hailakandi
8. Samarjit Choudhury, editor, Jugashakti, Karimganj, Assam was interviewed on Dec 2004 at Jugashakti Press, Karimjanj
9. H. R. Choudhuty, editor, Navabarta Prasanga, Karimganj, Assam was interviewed on 29th Dec 2004 at Nababarta Prakashan, Karimjanj
10. Partha Bhattacahjee, editor, Prasagik Kichu Katha, Silchar, Assam was interviewed on 30th Jan 2005 at Prasongik Press, Silchar
11. Paritosh Paul Choudhuty, a veteran journalist and an Activist of Language Movement Silchar, was interviewed on 26th June 2004 at Subhas Nagar, Silchar
12. Santanu Ghose, editor of Jugashankha and Senior Correspondent of 'The Telegraph' Silchar, was interviewed on 28th January 2005 at Nazirpatty, Silchar.

REFERENCES

Bhattacharjee Amalendu, 1982. *'Barak Upatyakar Sahityer Itihass Rachana Prasanga' Aksharbritta*, Ist year.

Bhattacharjee, Bijit Kumar 2000 *Atandra O Barak Upatakaya, Bangla* Kayaba Charcha, Hailakandi: Sihatiya Prakashan

Bhattacharjee, Bijit Kumar 2002 *Uttar Purva Bharater Bangla Sahitiya,* Hailakandi: Sihatiya Prakashan

Bhattacharjee, J.B. 1986 *Studies in The History of North-East India,* Shillong: Publication.

Bhattacharjee, Jatin Mohan 1942 *Srihattabashi Sampadiya Abong,* Srihatta O Cachar Haite Prakashito Sambad Patrika, Syleth: Bangladesh

Bhattacharjee, Usharanjan 1993 *Srihatta Sahitya Parishat O Patrika,* Calcutta: Oriental Publishers.

Das, Atin 1998 *Satabdir Taithya Punji, Barak Upatakaya Banga Sahitya Sambelan,* Silchar: Prasongik Printers and Publication.

Das, Kaliprasana 1964 *Sambadpatra Sebay Srihatter Sthan*, Shillong.

Paul Choudhury Paritosh 2002 *Raktanjalli* Matribhumi Press, Silchar.

8

The Barak Valley in the Contemporary Time

To motivate the people for action, the vernacular press has more opportunity to act and respond to the aspirations of the people of different provinces. The social reform movement facilitated the growth of the vernacular press in different parts of the country. Therefore, the vernacular press has had more influence on the people of a particular region. It could do what Anglo-Indian and Indo-Anglican press could not Newspapers have been published, on large scale from every corner since, the first-one, the publication of the first newspaper "Silchar", in 1886 in Silchar.

At present, in all, six dailies are published from the Barak Valley. Besides, there are also published the periodicals like bi-weekly, weekly and fortnightly.

The six dailies are 'Dainik Jugashankha', 'Dainik Sonar Cachar', 'Dainik Samayik Prasanga', 'Dainik Gati', 'The Frontier Sun' and The Silchar Times. A synoptic view of the particulars of select daily newspapers is given in Table 8.1.

Table 8.1 shows that the six dailies have originated in Silchar town from 1950 to 1994. Three newspapers : namely Jugashankha, Sonar Cachar and Samayik Prasanga is contain eight pages. Gati and frontier Sun contain six pages, and one newspaper namely Silchar Time contains four pages. The price the first three papers are Rs 3/- each ;of the next two papers are Rs 2/- each and of the last one is Re 1.50/-. They indicate only slight variations in their and print area and in the matter of columns they show a similarity. But in the matter of circulation Jugashankha topped the list followed by the Sonar Cachar. 'Silchar Times' has the lowest circulation and the remaining three have the in- between circulation.

All but one paper is published in Bengali language. All of these have originated in Silchar Town. If taken the total circulation of the newspapers it appears quite significant in the given size of the population and the literacy ratio in the valley.

When the circulation of this newspapers are looked through their distribution in the valley, it reveals some spatial patterns. The circulation in the district is shown in Table 8.2.

Table 8.1 shows that except the 'Dainik Samayik Prasanga' all the newspapers have the highest circulation in Cachar district as it is also a largest district in terms of population. In the circulation Jugashankha topped in all but Karimjanj district. Outside the valley the English daily, Frontier Sun, has a circulation more than any Bengali daily. It is apparent that the Bengali dailies have the most circulation among the Bengali speaking in the valley and the English daily has a very significant level of circulation among the non Bengali speaking people outside the valley.

To understand the status of the contemporary press in the Barak Valley, some cases of the press publication are studied in this chapter.

SILCHAR TOWN

Dainik Prantajyoti[1]

Serving the downtrodden and fighting for justice are the ideas that Jyotirindra Chandra Dutta, the founder editor of 'Dainik Prantajyoti' have nurtured in his heart and mind since

Table 8.1: Particulars of the Selected Daily Newspaper in Barak Valley

Sl. No.	Name of Newapaper	Started	Pages	Price	Size	Prtint Area	No. of Colums	Circula-tion	Language	Origi-nating centre
1.	Jugashankha	1950	08	3.00	54×38	52cm	08	49,579	Bengali	Silchar
2	Sonar Cachar	1978	08	3.00	54×38	52cm	08	46,000	Bengali	Sichar
3	Samyik Prasanga	1978	08	3.00	56×38	54cm	08	38,000	Bengali	Silchar
4	Gati	1968	06	2.00	50×36	48cm	08	31500	Bengali	Silchar
5	Silchar Times	1994	04	1.50	50×30	50cm	08	14227	Bengali	Silchar
6	Fronier Sun	1985	06	2.00	54×36	52cm	08	27,000	English	Silchar

Source : *INS Book 2004 and DIPR, Cachar.

his childhood. It was just the lack of ample opportunity that Dutta could not put into practice his noble ideas. The case was simple enough. He had an urge, and tendency but the right time did not strike. A hearth was already prepared, waiting for ignition.

Yes, the hearth was ignited but through Dutta's personal tragedy. Tragedy struck one night when one of Sri Dutta's cousin sisters, Smt. Purabi Dutta fell, seriously ill. The incident took place on 18th December 1956. At the dead of night Dutta in panic and grief went in search of timely medical help. But, unfortunately, his request was turned down by the doctors who were approached for help. For them, it was not convenient to come out in the late hours. At last, the pleas and requests of Dutta went unheard. He lost his sister that very night. This episode left him shattered. But then time he firmly decided to expose the callousness of the doctors. The decision was executed through "Jyoti" which was started on 12th January 1957 as a fortnightly in Silchar. He was himself the editor of the paper.

The title 'Jyoti' of the newspaper was short-lived. The Registrar of Newspapers in India (RNI) asked him to change the name as there was already a newspaper of the same title being published from Vardhaman (West Bengal). Then, the name "Prantajyoti" was decided. And the word "Prantajyoti", according to Sri Dutta, meant *the light of the eastern region.* Literally, "Prantajyoti" means **the light of the land**. He wanted to bring light in the eastern corner of India through a newspaper like 'Prantajyoti'. Every institution or organization has its own motto. The motto and editorial policy of the paper, "Dainik Prantajyoti", according to its all time editor, Sri Jyotrindra Chandra Dutta is to serve the society. It also aimed at fighting against corruption and injustice. Sri Dutta since his school days was greatly inspired by the ideals of Swami Vivekananda. It was therefore a golden opportunity for him to incorporate those ideas in his newspaper. Sri Jyotirindra Chandra Dutta believes that a newspaper reflects what is going on in a society. This is the way he thinks, he informs and at the same time

Table 8.2: Press Circulation in Barak Valley

Sl. No.	Daily Newspaper	Cachar	Karimganj	Hailakandi	Others
1	Dainik Jugashankha	30,000	10,000	9000	1243
2	Dainik Sonar Cachar	24,000	13,500	5,500	3000
3	Dainik Samayik Prasanga	11,400	11,400	14,000	1,200
4	Dainik Gati	10,000	6,000	3,300	200
5	Dainik Silchar Times	7000	4000	3000	227
6	The Frontier Sun	12,500	6,000	2,000	6,500

Source: INS Book 2004 and DIPR, Cachar.

educates and involves the members of the society in the service of the fellow members.

According to Dutta, within a short span after Independence, our country started facing various problems - corruption being one of them. Informing the people about the fact, he thought he could fight the corruption effectively. He believes that *'Pen is mightier than sword'* The 'Dainik Prantajyoti' disclosed illegal deeds of many corrupt public figures and officials, irrespective of their high status or position.

One great contribution of Sri Jyotirindra Chandra Dutta was in the arena of upliftment of women. That time no women was employed in the press in Silchar. He was the first person to employ women in the press. He personally taught them composition and hand-printing. He thought that for raising the position of women in society, they primarily required economic independence.

In the initial stage when the newspaper was published as fortnightly, its size was like any other small indigenous newspaper. The problem was that the newspaper did not have its own press and was printed at others press. The newspaper became a weekly in 1958. But the condition of its printing could not improve.

During the time of language movement in 1961 it adopted an extraordinary method of disseminating the day-to-day incidents. It started coming out in the post-card size and gave news in just one or two lines. It saved space and was more convenient. From the time of language movement, Sri Dutta felt the need of a daily newspaper. He started publishing it as a daily newspaper, title "Dainik Prantajyoti".

The Barak Valley is dominated by Bengali speaking people. The people of this Valley had the right to speak, read and write in Bengali. But in 1961, the Bimala Prasad Chaliha ministry tried to impose Assamese as the medium of instruction in the schools. The whole valley protested against this circular. The days were full of incidents and people were eager to know these incidents and their consequences. The people were in need of a newspaper that could at least give the basic and up-to-date information. The "Dainik Prantajyoti" catered to the needs.

The main contribution of the newspaper to the language movement is that it disseminated the updated, important and brief news in the general public. This was not done by any other newspaper at that time. It was the first daily newspaper in the north-east region. Its contribution in the language movement was particularly significant as it became a 'daily 'only during the movement in 1961.

A paper which had once great popularity is now facing a teething problem of financial crunches. Recently, in a local daily newspaper it appeared that the editor of "Prantojyoti" is seeking for some donation from the people. The paper's editor Sri Jyotirnindra Chandra Dutta attributes the lack of modernized printing techniques as one of the prime reasons for its present sorry state. He says that shortly time offset printing facilities will be made and the dream that Dutta has cherished will be realized. He says that the paper is trying to regain its lost popularity and circulation.

Dainik Sonar Cachar[2]

'Dainik Sonar Cachar' is a very popular newspaper of the Barak Valley. 'Sonar Cachar' was first published on 8th May 1978 under the editorship of Ranobir Roy. It became daily on 26th January 1979 and was named as 'Dainik Sonar Cachar'. Mr. Roy was involved with many burning news and also worked as a social worker. This background influenced his journalism. He founded a press, 'Sonar Cachar'. It was first published from its own press, which was at Nivedita lane, Hailakandi Road. And now, it is shifted to Shillongpatty. At the very beginning its circulation was poor.

At present, Mrs. Anita Roy is the editor of 'Dainik Sonar Cachar'. In September 2003 Mr. Ranobir Roy was brutally murdered in his own school campus. There are some newspapers under it. Among them, 'Apanjan' was started as a Daily Bengali newspaper in 1993 under the editorship of Pijush Kanti Das. But it wound up in 1995 due to some reasons.

"Dainik Sonar Cachar" has the printing area of 52cm/ 8 columns. The width of each column is 4.5cm. Its present circulation is 44653. It is priced Rs 3/-. The main contents are related to politics, business, environment, popular science, social interest, and literary and cultural news. The area of news coverage is urban, local, regional, national, and international. It gives preference to the news according to its depth. At present it has become a popular daily because of the use of modern technology in collection and printing of news.

It has its correspondents in the vital places like the capital cities of the north eastern states, Calcutta, Delhi, Mumbai, Chennai, Bangalore and Dhaka. It has acquired the modern technology of receiving news through fax, telex, telephone, Internet, etc. It has also multi color printing facility. It started the Internet facility in September 1998.

It gets advertisements mainly through various advertisement agencies. The growth rate of advertisement is 17%. Dainik Sonar Cachar has got Audit Bureau certificate of its advertisement.

Its editorial policy aims to constructive and fearless writing. There is no question of any compromise. It has always an impartial attitude towards the society. It was an eminent newspaper in the region, its editorial policy purports to bring about great awareness among the people of the society.

It is mainly circulated in Assam, Meghalaya, Arunachal Pradesh, Manipur, Tripura, Nagaland, West Bengal and Bangladesh.

About the 'Sonar Cachar' one way say : "Last in, first Out" means that the paper which started a few years ago (in 1978) but has gained popularity very shortly. Sonar Cachar is one of the talented and influential local newspapers of Silchar. It is was one of the most informative and motivating local newspapers. It has been found that after adopting the modern technology like off set printing, internet, etc. it has got popularity. Besides, its editorial policy of the fearless writing, constructive writing has also contributed to its popularity.

Dainik Jugashankha[3]

'Jugashankha' started in December 17, 1950 was a weekly newspaper. Its publisher and editor, Baidyanath Nath, was a famous teacher who subsequently joined the freedom movement. Earlier, in 1948, started a newspaper, 'Mukti Prodip'. 'Jugasankha' was published from the Modern Press, Central Road, Silchar. It was a crown sized paper, printed in letter press machine. The modern press was owned by somebody else. Therefore, Baidyanath Nath had to work very hard to publish this paper. This weekly newspaper called 'Jugashankha' followed the Congress ideology. Though it was a weekly publication, the paper could not be published it regularly. Besides this newspaper among its contemporary newspapers 'Prantojyoti' was an important one. Mr. Nath died in the year 1970. Then his son Bijoy Krishna Nath, took the responsibility. In 1971, their own press was established in Rongpur. In the same year, it became the first circulation based weekly newspaper in the valley. It was the first paper in the Barak Valley, which really thought of its target readers. At distribution level also, 'Jugasankha' created the renaissance in the region. This paper was systematically distributed by chain of hawkers at all the railway station book shops and the wheelers in Lumding - Silchar train route. It not only increased its readers in Silchar, Hailakandi, Karimganj, Lala Bazar, Dwarbond, Sonai and Algapur. But also created its circulation in the remote places like North Cachar Hills, Maibong, Haflong and Jatinga. It changed its shape from 'Crown Size' to 'Demy size' which was regularly published on every Friday. The 'Jugasankha' created enthusiasm among the masses who eagerly waited for the newspaper.

During the Bhasa Andolon in 1960-61, the 'Jugasankha' played a very important role to cover the news about the movement and to inspire the local people against the Assamese dominance. This weekly condemned the police firing on the

Satyagrahis on 19th May 1961, which resulted into the killing of eleven Satyagrahis.

At the time of Bangladesh operation in 1971 'Jugasankha' played a very vital role in communication of message. It published numerous articles to show the Government path of victory against Pakistan and to eliminate the them East Pakistan.

In the meantime, 'Jugasankha' became bi-weekly newspaper and then in 1982 it converted into a daily newspaper. A group of youth and talented writers like Atin Das, Anadi Chakraborty, Jishu Chanda and others got associated with it. In 1983, the newspaper shifted to Guwahati and started publishing as the first Bengali daily there. Besides, 'Dainik Ahom' (an Assamese daily newspaper), it was the second newspaper published on sheet page and in four to six pages. In 1989 its publication was suspended after of a fire incident which destroyed all the machinery of the press.

After the fire incident, the kit was started on off-set printing in higher press. Subsequently, it had to suspend its publication in view of some financial problems. In 1994, it was revived from a letter press owned by Atin Das in Silchar. On 9th May 1995 it resumed its publication on offset painters with computerized composing. Bijoy Krishna Nath was the editor and Atin Das, the Executive Editor. The total project including offset printing machinery costed Rupees One crore and 20 lakhs. The 'Assam Financial Corporation' extended to it the financial assistance. In April 1996, Atin Das became the editor of Dainik 'Jugasankha'. Since then it never looked back. It has become the 'numero uno' newspaper in the region. Atin Das is a dynamic and versatile personality who has a very attitude towards the modern professional journalism. He is a staunch follower of the journalists like Satyen Mazumder, editor of 'Jugantor' and Bibekananda Mukhopadhay. He was also greatly influenced by Tofojjul Hussain, the editor of largest circulated newspaper in Bangladesh, 'Dainik Ittefaq'. In his early life, Atin Das used to write for 'Dainik Ittefaq'. Due to his able guidance and professional outlook he brought a major change in the production and distribution of 'Dainik Jugasankha'.

The Jugasankha Group of Publications conducted a readership survey of target consumers to make a new managerial policy. In May 1995, their circulation was merely 3000 copies while their target was to reach 10,000 readers. But within a period of six months they have sold 15,000 copies in the valley. This is a five times increase, which is beyond their expectation. In Karimganj, its circulation increased from 500 to 6000 copies within a given time.

Due to the tremendous growth of 'Jugasankha' circulation of the Bengali newspapers from Calcutta faced a heavy setback in the valley. They lost 50% of their circulation in Silchar, 70% in Karimganj/Hailakandi and almost 100% in North Cachar Hills. Now, 'Dainik Jugasankha' is the most circulated Bengali newspaper in the North East. According to an unofficial source of the paper, it has they have crossed the circulation mark of 30,000 copies.

"Fear none, favour none" is the main motto of 'Jugasankha'. Objectivity and credibility play important role in determining their editorial policy. It contains articles on political and literary matters. Its articles are strictly against rampant corruption done of the government officials and political leaders. The 'Dainik Jugasankha' has been often critical of the ruling party. It always made a distinction between programmes and measures, on the one side, and the personalities and parties, on the other. Their criticism has been primarily against the non-wisdom or inappropriateness of the policies or decisions of a government in power. It will continue to judge them by professionalism and performance.

With the increased circulation and greater influence among the people, 'Dainik Jugasankha' critically looked into the affairs of administration during the Bhasa Andolon. It played an influential role and created a mass movement against the administration. At the time of Bangladesh operation it showed the Government a right path and inspired the masses to fight against Pakistan by contributing to the will power and mental attitude of the 'Mukti Joddha Bahini'.

As a living example of professional journalism, 'Jugasankha' continues to serve the public upholding the ideals of independence, democracy and secularism and holding its head high against all forms of communalism and parochialism.

Jugashankha's style is simple but effective. Its readers are mostly middle class and lower middle class people, a large portion of which reside in the villages. It uses simple words and short sentences to deliver the message to the masses. People from all over the valley eagerly wait for the newspaper every morning.

Barak Valley lacks a proper infrastructure for newspaper production. Transport and communication is one of the barriers in a smooth circulation of the newspapers. Then, the newsprints from Russia, China, and Canada cannot reach here on time due to poor condition of transport facility. Serious obstacle to the development of press in Barak Valley is per capita income of the readers. They cannot buy newspaper every day. Secondly and most importantly, illiteracy is also a considerable factor behind it

Newspapers cannot run without advertisements. It hampers the publication of newspapers. Without advertisement the proprietors are bound to face financial problems. Lack of advertisements and shrinkage of market have made the press of the valley backward. But the Jugasankha Group of Publication tries to stand against all the odds. They were publishing an English economic daily, 'Oil Field Times' from Guwahati. But now it is not running. They have their special correspondents spread in the few cities of the country. Using modern technology, 'Jugasankha' has started the magazination of which is very popular and other newspapers have also introduced it. 'Jugasankha' started various sections for sports, children, women, etc. in the newspapers. It conducts debates on various sensitive issues. In the last Lok Sobha elections they conducted the opinion poll and created a sensation in the valley. It has built its various departments; viz., advertisement, circulation and editorial. It has opened a 'matrimonial' section and is wholeheartedly greeted by the people. To get more advertisements, 'Jugashankha' has set up its advertisement offices at different places in India. Recently, 'Jugashankha' has started publication in colour printing.

The newspaper industry in Barak Valley is facing so many hurdles. But they are confident, they believe in their duty to disseminate ideas to the farthest corner of the valley.

KARIMGANJ TOWN

Case Study: Jugashakti[4]

The 'Jugashakti' is the oldest weekly newspaper of the Karimganj District, the history of which dates back to the pre-Independence period. It was established by Subodh Chandra Dutta in 1936. The management of this paper was in the hand of a Trustee Board consisted of the members like Abala Kanta Gupta and Basant Kumar Das. It was then published from Sarada Press owned by Digendra Nath Dev. In 1945 the ownership of the paper went to Bidhu Bhushan Chowdhury. He was the editor of the paper. In 1974 after his death, the charge of the paper was taken up by his son, Samarjit Chowdhury, the present editor.

Its Guwahati edition came in 1971 largely due to the personal initiative of Rabijit Chowdhury, a noted journalist and writer of the Barak Valley. However, due to financial constraints and other problems the paper could not continue more than four years. Rabijit Chowdhury was instrumental even in starting its daily edition from Silchar in 1981. It was published from Sarada Press and Publication Pvt. Ltd., with Rabijit Chowdhury was its editor. However, due to financial crisis it could not survive more than a year.

At present, only the weekly version of 'Jugashakti' is in operation. It is being published from the 'Sree Jugashakti Press' established in 1991. However, it has become to a one-man venture of Samarjit Chowdhury who is its editor, reporter, proof reader, etc., all in one. The present circulation of the paper is approximately 4000 copies per issue.

Navabharata Prasanga[5]

'Navabharata Prasanga' the only bi-weekly Bengali newspaper of Karimganj comes regularly on every Tuesday and Friday. The paper first came out on April 12, 1986 as a weekly newspaper. It became bi-weekly on 7th September 1992. The paper is being published by Navabarta Prakashan, Karimganj, owned, and edited by Habibur Rahman Choudhury.

On 11th July 1985 the paper carried out some writings against the government. At that time it was not registered under RNI. So, the then Deputy Commissioner of the Karimganj district, D.N. Bhattacharjee ordered the publisher to stop publication of the paper. The paper went into hibernation until it was revived on April 24, 1986.

The paper secured the approval of the Government of Assam for release of Government advertisement in 1992. It was approved by the Government of India in the year 1995.

The 'Navabharata Prasanga' has brought out special issues from time to time at regular intervals. The issues like the 'Navabarta Sharadia' special published in 1990 and 1991 and the Navabarata Idd special in 1987, 1989, 1990, 1993 are worth mentioning. On 15th August 1992 there came a special issue on the freedom fighters of both Surma and Brahmaputra valley. The issue carried two special articles *"August Biplbe Akhanda Syleter Bhumika"* by Nikunja Behari Goswami of Sylhet (Bangladesh) and *"Fashir Mancha Surma Upatakar Pratham Shahid Asit Bhattacharjee"* by Nisith Ranjan Das, Ex MLA and Vice Principal of Badarpur College. It also contained the profiles of the martyrs like Makhan Lal Paul, Maulana Jalal Uddin, Manish Bhattacharjee of the Barak and the Surma Valley and Kanaklata Barua, Vogeswari Fukaneni, Madan Rowta, N. Rajbangshi, Kushual Kuor and others.

A Souvenir, 'Smaranika', was also published to comme-morate the freedom fighter Netaji on the Netaji Mela and Exhibition on

1990, 1991,1992 and 1997. Two souvenirs: namely, 'Rangali' on the occasion of Rangali Bihu and, 'Samannay' on the occasion of Assam Sahitya Sabha Conference in 1991,1992 and 1993.

At present, the average circulation of this paper is 10,650. The target readers of the paper are the people residing in the immediate vicinity of the town. The paper has got its readers in the West Asian countries, namely, Saudi Arabia, Kuwait, Iran and Abu Dhabi. The basic purpose of this paper is to bring into focus the news of local interest. It basically deals with rural news.

The Challenger Barta[6]

The Challenger Barta, the only English newspaper of Karimganj District, came into being on 28th February 1994. The paper has been a weekly. Since its inception. After the two years of its inception, the paper was approved by the DAVP, the state government and the railways as an advertiser. The paper introduces B.G's column that has extended as an navigating young talent to come up with their creative words in its publication.

The average circulation of the paper is 3980. As has been estimated during the period from 1/1/97 to 31/12/97 its circulation in rural areas is 2380 while in urban areas it is 1420.

The paper was started with a view to chiefly serve the requirement of the non-Bengali reading public of the district. So, it caters to the reading requirement of the people of the area residing inside and outside district. The paper provides an opportunity to upcoming educated youths to write articles, features, etc. to publish it. It tries to provide a forum for the young generation to manifest their talent by publishing stories, poems, etc.

MAGAZINE PUBLICATION FROM SILCHAR

Prasangik Kichhu Katha[7]

The magazine,' Prasangik Kichu Katha' was started in January 1994 by the name of 'Prasangik'. Two working journalists of the Sentinel Group of Newspaper, Guwahati, Partha Bhattacharjee and Arijit Aditya, co-edited the magazine. The 'Prasangik Kichhu Katha' was allotted by the Registrar of Newspapers of India, New Delhi, in 1996. Initially, the magazine used to be published from Guwahati and its publication was not regular. 'Prasangik Kichhu Katha' was a purely commercial magazine formally launched on 2nd August 1998 in Silchar. Apart from Bhattacharjee and Aditya, Sri Bijit Chowdhury, veteran journalist of the valley, also took the charge of chief editor. Himashish Bhattacharjee was the honorary news editor. The Guwahati correspondents were Amal Gupta and Aminur Rahman.

Initially, the magazine was an amateur venture. Utter absence of a magazine in Bengali in Assam prompted the editors to take the plunge. The encouraging response received strengthened their confidence. The vast demand for an out and out commercial Bengali magazine in Assam, particularly the Barak Valley, which would cater to the sentiments and aspirations of the Bengali speaking people, finally, inspired them to bring out "Prasangik Kichhu Katha' as a purely commercial magazine. It was an endeavour to focus on various socio-political problems and to search for their positive solution.

The magazine aimed at focusing on the socio-political issues of the region. The cover story in every issue reflected to the basic aim of solving socio-cultural problem of the region. The first cover story of the news version of the magazine was about the silent revolution of the Muslim women of Barak Valley. The last issue is about the plight of the road and transport system. Apart from the cover story, the index was characterized with certain regular features concerning cultural activities, poems, short stories, dramas, sports, women's health, interview of a prominent figure, state politics debate on socio-political issues. The magazine proudly published two regular columns written by two eminent figures; viz., Dr. Partha Chattopadhya and Dr. Sujit Chowdhury.

So far as the editorial policy is concerned, the magazine aimed at focusing on the various socio-political problems with a search for positive solution. Strictly avoiding any sort of mud-slinging, the magazine tries to offer a platform for exchange of opinion. To bridge the gap between the two valleys as well as among various communities in the state was another feature that the magazine tried to emphasise on.

As magazine journalism is not a well known practice in the region, it is the 'Prasangik Kichhu Katha' which tried to create such a practice by incorporating news-oriented views of the various quarters. It requires in-depth analysis of a particular incident or trend. So far as society is concerned, the magazine claimed dedication for over all development of the valley in particular and the state as a whole. It tried to highlight various problems faced by society. In its first issue, the cover story about the Muslim women's positive in the valley. It tried to make the women aware about their legal rights.

In 2001, 3000 copies were printed every month. After that it stopped its publication. During the period, it primarily worked better in the urban areas of the valley as well as in Guwahati. However, the letters from the villages also make it clear that it has a potential among the rural readership. The first issue having an article on the Muslim women evoked good response in Muslim dominated rural areas like Patherkandi, Sonai, etc. Due to non-cooperation from books' agents in Silchar town and non-availability of wide marketing network the magazine could not survive.

HAILAKANDI TOWN

Dibakar[8]

This newspaper was started as a weekly in the year 1980. It was published from a small town Lala of Hailakandi district. Its editor was Abdul Kalam Mazumdar. It played a great role in motivating young journalist of Hailakandi district to take the challenge of the profession. This paper used to come with very good writings in the district

In the 1980s, numerous publications of newspaper flooded the Hailakandi district was flooded with so many newspapers. But none of them exists today except one or two and Dibakar is one of them. Still it is continuing with a good readership. Now it is registered to Government of Assam. The present editor is Mrs. Aleya Mazumder. A scanned copy of the front page of the paper is shown here.

In sum, the press in Barak Valley, particularly the newspapers, are continuing to shape and mould the destiny of the valley through information and education. It is continuing as effective and economical medium for awareness creating and advertising. Image building, opinion moulding and attitudinal changes cannot achieve success without the press. Therefore, the press is of paramount significance to achieve both commercial goal and social objectives. It is well evident that there appear and re-appear newspapers and magazines in the valley, yet there sustained only a small number of these. But publication entrepreneurship itself is a symbol of the consciousness among the people in the valley.

NOTES

1. Jatindra Chandra Dutta, the founder editor of *Danik Prantajyoti*, Silchar was interviewed 24nd September 2004 at Prantojyoti Office, Silchar
2. Mridul Roy, the Editor, *the Frontier Sun*, Silchar was interviewed on 14th December 2004 at Sonar Cachar Press, Silchar
3. Atin Das, a veteran journalist and ex editor of *Jugashankha*, Silchar, was interviewed on 30th September 2004 at Rongpur, Silchar
4. Samarjit Choudhury, editor, *Jugashakti*, Karimganj, was interviewed on 29th December 2004 at Jugashakti Press, Karimjanj
5. H. R. Choudhuty, the editor, *Navabarta Prasanga*, Karimganj, was interviewed on 29th December 2004 at Nababarta Prakashan, Karimjanj

6. B.G. Bhattacharjee, the editor, *Challenger Barta*, Karimganj, was interviewed on 29th December 2004 at Nababarta Prakashan, Karimjanj
7. Partha Bhattacahjee, editor, the *Prasagik Kichu Katha*, Silchar, was interviewed on 30th January 2005 at Prasongik Press, Silchar
8. Nitish Bhattacharjee, editor, the *Purbayan*. Hailakandi, Assam was interviewed on 16th January 2005 at S.S. College, Hailakandi.

9

Socio-Economic Impacts of the Barak Valley Press

Society is divided into different strata. In the stratification the lower and middle section always remain indifferent to various developments in society. In the pre-Independence India there was a hindrance to the avouchment of people against British rule. The press served them detailed information and tenets and targets of freedom movement. In this way press has a tremendous effect on the people of Barak Valley.Besides the women in our society remain in backward state. The press helped the women directly and indirectly to come out of shackles and join the main line activities of the society.In brief everywhere in the world and particularly in this part of the country the press took a leading role to impart the education and gave the information to the people to make their choice in social affairs.

Development Issues

Though Barak Valley is free from the ill-effects of caste and creed, even then its social backwardness and economic stagnation have stood in the way of its systematic and scientific development. It is the press which has, exposed the immediate and imperative needs of social and economic packages for evaluating the emotion of people in several sections particularly marginalized people. It would be exaggeration to say that the treatment meted out to this valley by the successive governments at Shillong and Dispur has been constantly brought to the by the media. Eventaully, the attitudes of the government did change. Notwithstanding the country's aberration in respect of allocation of funds, to the valley, it is sustained campaign by the local press that it has brought about significant change. Today, this scenario has changed, the funds for various developments and schemes, projects are forthcoming. A change can be observed in the sense that the disparity and level of poverty have substantially come down. Despite the spectre of poverty, the target people, i.e the marginalized sections have now ample opportunities through the rural development programmes and schemes. It is the press which prime responsibility is to improve the communication without whom the economic development of the valley cannot be ensured. National highways, agriculture, the construction as well as the expectations of road networks are the result of the sustained campaign by the press.

The press has launched campaigns to highlight the socio-economic conditions are as follows:

1. Pineapple Juice Processing Plant at Fulertal
2. Pineapple Concentrate Plant
3. Cold Storage at Mashimpur
4. Badarpur Textile Mill
5. Cachar Sugar Mill
6. CAMUL
7. H.P.C
8. Tea Industry
9. University

The data reveal from Table 9.1 that the Dainik Jugasankha and the Sonar Cachar have given almost equal emphasis with regard to the coverage of various developmental schemes and programmes included in the study.

The analysis of the news contents regarding these developmental issues is undertaken here. Newspapers are an important medium and a very potent means of communication to the masses. It is unfortunate that hardly 20% of the six daily newspapers in the valley contain agricultural news and that, too, covers only 0.18% to 3% of their total news coverage.This means that a small fraction of the news relevant to the rural readers reachas the villages of the valley where the rural people constitute 80% its total population.When analysed the contents of the farm magazine, the most important determinant of the success of press it has an attractive cover page and format but without the timely, need-based and locally relevant content.

In the year 2003-04 the IRDP received 4% to 5% coverage in the newspapers. Of the papers, the Dainik Jugasankha has given the maximum coverage of (5.0%) on IRDP the other papers giving the coverage are the Sonar Cachar (4.7%), the Samayik Prashanga(4.5% each), the Silchar Times(4.0%), the Gati (4.2%) and the Frontier Sun(3.9%).

The analyses, of the newspapers indicate that they have given very marginal coverage to agricultural news, i.e., varying from 0.18 % to 2.74 % with an average of 1.44 %. The coverage by the newspapr of various development issues is presented in the following table.

Table 9.1 presents the data about the coverage of the development news and issues in the six newspapers;namely, the Dainik Jugasankha (49.5 %), the Dainik Sonar Cachar (49.4 %), the Samayik Prashanga (47.6 %), the Silchar Times (41.9 %), the Gati (44.2 %) and the Frontier Sun (41.5%).

To assess the impact of the press in Barak Valley with regard to various socio-economic developments programmes initiated during 2003-2004, there were interviewed the cross sections of the people in each district of the Barak valley. It

Table 9.1: Development Issues Reported in the Newspapers (28-09-2003 to 27-09-2004)

Item	Juga-shankha	Sonar Cachar	Samayik Prashanga	Silchar Times	Gati	Frontier Sun
Twenty Point Programme	3.1	3.0	3.1	2.7	2.9	2.6
Integrated Rural Development Programme	5.0	4.7	4.5	4.0	4.2	3.9
Family Planning, Health and Hygiene	3.9	4.0	4.0	3.0	3.3	3.2
Agricultural Development	4.0	3.8	4.0	3.3	3.1	3.3
Irrigation and Drinking water	3.6	3.3	3.1	3.0	3.5	3.0
Educational Development	3.4	3.6	3.8	3.0	3.1	2.9
Scientific, Technological & Industrial Dev.	4.3	4.0	3.8	3.6	3.7	3.4
Energy & Power	2.6	2.2	2.4	2.0	2.1	2.1
SCs & STs	3.9	4.1	4.0	3.5	3.8	3.4
Children & women Welfare	3.0	3.2	2.9	2.8	2.9	2.9
Youth Welfare & Development	3.3	3.5	3.5	3.0	3.1	2.9
Social Welfare	3.2	3.6	3.0	2.9	2.7	

Source: Content Analysis of Dainik Jugashankha, Dainik Sonar Cachar, Dainik Samayik Prasanga, Dainik Gati, Dainik Silchar Times and The Frontier Sun. from 28th Sept 2003 to 27th Sept 2004

is found that these programmes are appreciated by the people of the area. The study reveals the following facts:

1. In Cachar District, 56% of the people interviewed have appreciated the role and impact of the press in respect of these programmes.The impact of the press and the programmes have brought about social change. 33% people have criticized these programmes and 6% people remained neutral.
2. In Karimganj district, 59.5 % people have appreciated the role of the press and programmes ; 29% people criticized the role and 11.5 % people were neutral.
3. In Hailakandi, 57.5 % people appreciated the role, 30.5 % people criticized the role and 12% people were neutral in this regard.

Briefly, a majority of the people appreciated the role of the press in reporting and communicating the people about various development programmes.

Agricultural Reporting

The main source of livelihood of the people of Barak Valley is agriculture. To understand the material condition of the people of the valley, it is attempted to know the sources relating to the state of agriculture during the colonial regime through the documents like the Census of India, 1911 (vol. iii, Assam), Census of India 1921 (vol. iii, p.1), Report on the Annual Revenue Adminstation of Cachar 1871-72, and Cachar Records. Besides these, some other sources like W.W. Hunter's. 'A Statistical Account of Assam', vol ii (Cambridge 1879), B.C. Allen's, 'Assam District Gazetteers', vol I (Allahabad 1905), 'The Imperial Gazetteers' of India, vol. ix, (London1908) and J.B. Bhattacharjee's, 'Cachar Under British Rule in North East India' (1977) are very useful in this connection.

Rice was the main crop of the valley. The green crops grown in Cachar were mustard, linseed, assort of pulse or kalai. hamp and jute were grown in small quantities for local consumption. From the various writings are can have the information regarding the stages of rice cultivation, area, turnout of crops and classification of land. About the position of the cultivator, these writings in Cachar settlement was Rayatwari. Under this system the revenue was collected directly from the Mirasdars. He also mentioned the agricultural implements used by the cultivators.

The staple crop in Cachar plains was rice which in 1903-04 covered 66% of the total cultivated area, oil seeds covered 5%, other foodgrains including pulses covered 1% and sugarcane covered 2%. Besides these, we get information regarding the raising of mustard, fibres and agricultural implements used by the cultivators.

In the field of agricultural, the reporting especially in of the rural development is fairly recent in Barak Valley. Studies under the umbrella of agricultural reporting have been going on in several Asian countries and the U.S.A with varying degrees of qualitative and quantitative emphasis. A review of the state-of-the art not only provides clues to certain facts and issues related to agricultural journalism in the past, but also directs the researchers in terms of the scope of journalism research for the near future.

The utility of findings from studies in the area of agricultural reporting (content analyses, readability, readership surveys, format studies, evaluation studies) have been viewed as marginal from the perspectives of media producers, policy makers and even the public. This observation, based on a review of agricultural journalism reporting in Barak Valley, is an indication of the limitations of the scope of agricultural journalism perceived so far by researchers

A survey of 50 randomly selected reporting of three local dailies having a bearing on agricultural reporting has been undertaken The coverage of the news in the newspapers is given here.

Table 9.2 shows that Dainik Jugashansha has given maximum coverage of 2.74, Dainik Sonar Cachar is given 2.60 coverage, Samayik Prasanga 2.08, Dainik Gati 1.20, Dainik

SilcharTimes is of 1.05 and minimum coverage has given Frontier Sun is of 0.18

Table 9.2: News on Agriculture

Newspaper	% Agriculture News
Danik Sonar Cachar	2.60
Samayik Prashanga	2.08
Silchar Times	1.05
Danik Gati	1.20
Danik Jogashankha	2.74
The Frontier Sun	0.18

Souces: Dainik Jugashankha, Dainik Sonar Cachar, Dainik Samayik Prasanga, Dainik Gati, Dainik Silchar Times and The Froniter Sun. from 28th Sept 2003 to 27th Sept 2004).

There were but four editorials (only carried none) and none of these accounted for more than 17.2 percent of the total column length. Only Dainik Jugashankha carried letters-to-the-editor on agriculture topics (three), accounting for 11.28 percent of its column length. However, an unequal number of issues were analyzed for each of the four newspapers. An average issue of Jugashankha carried 53 centimeters of agriculture content in its column, followed by Dainik Sonar Cachar (42cm), the Dainik Shamaik Prashanga(25.1cm), Dainik Gati (16.8cm), Dainik Silchar Times (10.5cm) and Frontier Sun (5cm) respectively.

The data in Table 9.2 and the preceding discussion clearly indicate that there is a pressing need for newspapers to devote more space to agricultural news. The majority of the newspapers gave almost their agricultural coverage to informative news. Opinion and educative agricultural news got less space

Social Welfare

In the Barak Valley the press has a role to play in the social welfare activities launched by the government. The objective of the social welfare activities is to increase the standard of life and living of various disadvantaged and deprived sections of the society. The government and other non-governmental organizations in India have to support these disadvantaged sections of the society because they are incapable of supporting themselves. Therefore, the govt. and other non-governmental organizations involved in the field of social welfare have to intervene to set right the situation.The broad term social welfare includes measures such as family planning, adult education, primary health care, and drinking water facilities undertaken by these bodies to promote the welfare of the citizens. In the process of development, the social welfare activities undertaken by the government and others play crucial role in the country. We need social welfare schemes to ameliorate the conditon of the under privileged sections of the society and to bring about prosperity to them.

The first and foremost organization, which carries out social welfare activities, is the government itself. The government through its Social Welfare Department.and the Central Board of Social Welfare carries out social welfare activities in the country.

These are the general roles performed by the press in social welfare. There are also certain specific roles that the media performed in select areas of social welfare activity. The press acts not only as the agent of information, change and persuasion but also as a force that gains with the public confidence and seeks co-operation from them.

The press in Barak Valley plays a crucial role of disseminating important information to people on social welfare. It not only informs the people but also persuades the people for their participation in the social welfare programmes launched with the objective of benefiting the under privileged.

Social welfare is an important aspect of the development in the valley, and the role played by press accelerates the process of acceptance of new ideas in social welfare. We know about many social welfares themes, not because of any thing else but only because of the press. They provide education and information to the people.

Table 9.3: Social Welfare News Coverage in the Newspapers

Newspaper	% Social welfare
Danik Jogashankha	18.2
Danik Sonar Cachar	17.2
Danik Samaik Prasangha	15.3
Danik Gati	10.2
Silchar Times	9.2
Frontier Sun	5.2

Source: Content Analysis of Dainik Jugashankha, Dainik Sonar Cachar, Dainik Samayik Prasanga, Dainik Gati, Dainik Silchar Times and The Froniter Sun. from 28th Sept 2003 to 27th Sept 2004)

Table 9.3 shows that Dainik Jugashansha has given the maximum coverage of 18.2, Dainik Sonar Cachar is given 17.2 coverage, Samayik Prasanga 15.3, Dainik Gati 10.2, Dainik SilcharTimes is of 9.2 and minimum coverage has given Frontier Sun is of 5.2. Thus, it appears that the press has created awareness among the people with regard to these welfare programmes.

From the analysis of the responses of the people interviewed, it is found that the press in Barak Valley moulded considerable public opinion in favour of different aspects of the Twenty Point Programme and Integrated Rural Development Programme which have raised the living standard of weaker sections of the people of the region through more employment generation, agricultural and industrial production and better health, environment, education and communication.

Tea Industry

One of the most remarkable innovations of the British rule in Cachar was to introduce the tea industry. Although primarily intended to serve the commercial aspirations of the British, the tea industry has completely changed the very face of the district through rapid socio-economic transformation.

Presently, Barak Valley tea industry is pleading for favourable treatment buy the state and the centre and for help overcome the impediments. The tea industry employs over 60, 000 thousand workers and other staff in the valley. The steady rise in prices of foodgrains under the Public Distribution System (PDS) makes things difficult. The tea gardens are under a contractual obligation to feed its labourers by supplying them subsidized rations comprising cereals and oil.

Both in the national and global markets, Barak Valley tea continues to wallow in ignominy as its products are looked down upon as "Common', though the produce of some gardens in Hailakandi district bordering Mizoram has the quality like that of Darjeeling tea. The packed CTC and green teas produced by some gardens have recently made a breakthrough in the market abroad, especially in Iran, Russia, Egypt and the UK.. The planters here are quite eager to grab the export market by impressing customers with quality.

During the period between December 2003 and December 2004, six dailies of the valley have been taken to analyze the news coverage they have given to tea industry.

Table 9.4 shows that The Silchar Times gave a more space to Tea Industry related news (52%) whereas Jugashankha and Samayik Prasanga gave it an equal coverage (40%each), Sonar Cachar gave 38% space, Gati gave 21% and The Frontier Sun gave 2% space of its news coverage to the news.

The problem of the tea gardens is compounded by poor telephone network.Planters are irked by low-voltage power in the gardens by the grid of Assam electricity board. The gardens will try to tap the growing market for packet tea, although the sick units will be hard put to meet the challenge given the paucity of funds at their disposal. Over 60 per cent of Barak Valley's 104 gardens are small and there fore prone to sickness.

Table 9.4: Tea Industry Coverage in the Newspapers

Dailies	Coverage
Dainik Jugashankha	40%
Dainik Sonar Cachar	38%
Dainik Samayik Prasanga	40%
Dainik Gati	21%
The Silchar Times	52%
The Frontier Sun	2%

Source: Dainik Jugashankha, Dainik Sonar Cachar, Dainik Samayik Prasanga, DainikGati, Dainik Silchar Times and The Froniter Sun. from 28th Sept 2003 to 27th Sept 2004.

Rural Development

The respondents expressed that socio-economic development of the poor, increasing agricultural production, creation of strong infrastructure in the rural areas and irrigation facilities are the important components of the rural development. They also maintain the programmes like distribution of land, providing of land, providing employment, construction and assignment of houses to the poor and upgradation of their skills are important for their development.

The analysis reveals that the impact of the press on rural development encompasses socio-economic development of the rural people, development of infrastructure, development of all categories of farmers, unity among people, responsive administration, elimination of social and cultural hurdles for development and higher level of consciousness of the people. The respondents said that the press in Barak Valley has mostly

Table 9.5: Views on the Impact of the Press on Rural Development in the Barak Valley (%)

Issues	Jugashankha Cachar	Sonar Prasanga	Samayik Times	Silchar	Gati	Frontier Sun
Development of Poor people	40	38	30	39	25	3
To increase agricultural production	30	30	25	10	12	2
Providing irrigation facilities	22	18	26	15	16	2
Providing loan houses to poor	35	30	28	10	12	0
Establishment of small scale industries	45	32	34	25	18	2
Providing employment to poor	34	39	24	21	10	1
Undertaking land development activities	10	10	12	9	7	0
Distribution of land to the poor	12	15	10	9	8	0
Supply of Electricity	49	47	38	32	22	4
Providing loans to the farmers	32	28	26	17	12	Nil
Creating infrastructure in the rural areas	39	34	29	14	10	2
Providing subsidies to all the farmers	23	20	22	39	17	Nil

Source: Interview of 50 eminent press personalities and journalist from three districts of Barak Valley.

favoured the development of the poor. The respondents also said that the press mostly favoured development of the poor and increasing agricultural production as the important aspects of rural development. However, some of the respondents have not expressed their opinion about rural development.

REFERENCES

Choudhury, Loho Biplap 1998 *NE Press fails to rise to occasion* Communicator: April-June.

Das, Atin 2002 Satabdir Taithya Punji Barak Upatakaya Banga Sahitya Sambelan Silchar: Prasongik Printers and Publication

Ghosh, Santanu 2003 *Development Committee ready to Basic Needs*, *The Telegraph*, 31st Oct.

Ghosh, Santanu 1999 *Derive on for Export highway*, *The Telegraph*, 19th July.

The Indian Newspaper Society 2004 INS Press Handbook, 2004.New Delhi: Indian Newspaper Society, Rafi Marg.

10

Summary, Findings and Conclusion

I

The Summary

The study is addressed to the question as to what kind of the historical evolution, i.e., the nature of origin, growth and development of the press during its historical evolution in the North Eastern region, specially in the Barak Valley of Assam state in India has undergone and what socio-historical and socio-contextual factors have conditioned the process. It aims at analysing and explaining the status of the Barak Valley press in its historical, professional and societal contexts.

As required by its nature, the descriptive research design has been used for collection and analysis of documentary, historical, oral and official data. The historical experiences and documents preserved with personalities and official establishments of press or otherwise form the crux of the information. The sources of data have been tapped comprehensively to analyze the contribution of the regional press to the process of nation-building and historical evolution of society. The study is placed in the context of the Barak Valley.

There have been lots of studies about the growth and development of the press in the Indian context. But there have been a few studies about the growth and development in the regional context in India. Barak Valley is the remotest area of Assam in North East India. There has been no studies related to the origin and development of press in the region, whereas it has contributed so many dailies and periodicals. But any systematic effort has not yet been made to reveal the background of journalism in Barak Valley except a few sketchy works. So this study was confined to know the status of Barak Valley journalism- its, origin, growth and development. On the occasion of 150 years celebration of Assam Journalism, one finds a special opportunity to throw light on the glorious róle played by the newspapers in the Barak Valley.

The valley is the region of biological, geographical and cultural diversities, contributing to the variegated character of North -Eastern region as a whole. Its demographic, social and cultural character make it distinct even within the North East. A very high rate of growth, density and in-migration of population, multi-ethnic, multi-lingual and multi-religious population, high literacy rate, multiple cultural activities, most peaceful place in the North-East ever growing trade activities and literary and journalistic activities, in all, make the region different from the rest. No doubt, the valley is resource-rich, but is also one of the country's most thickly populated areas. Its forest products, water resources, fruits and sugarcane yielding potential is yet to be utilized. As a land-scarce region of the country it needs appropriate planning and technology to ensure sustainable development. Srrounded in three sides by five out of the seven political units of the region and flanked by the Indo- Bangladesh international broder in the west the region assumes strategic importance alongwith other peculiarities to attract the national attention, on the one hand, and to deserve a guarantee of the linguistic and cultural identity linked with the question of development, on the other hand. Therefore, the demography, physiography, society, culture and politics have their role in shaping the press in the region. But the evolution of the press in general and the Indian press in particular has provided a historical background for the press in the valley.

The press travelling long from east to west got a fillip in the modern Europe and recieved great leap forward in the social conditions of the society in USA. While keeping an administrative objective in mind the British started the modern press in India, the leaders of the Indian freedom movement used the English and vernacular press in the pre-Independence as an effective means to propagate their message to the common people scattered far and wide in the country. After Independence, the press became one of the important means in the hands of political and intellectual leadership to disseminate the message in the masses for development and nation-building. It has come a long way since its humble beginning in the British period. Today, in India there are as many rural readers as urban. The readership of magazine, specially in urban India, has shown an encouraging uptrend over the years in the contemporary times. The press in Assam, like the Indian Press, has its original roots in the missionary efforts. In both the cases the origin is extraneous. The press in India was initiated by the missionaries and was brought up systematically by the British for their administrative needs whereas in Assam it emerged and developed through the Assamese language and literature under the efforts made by the missionaries. In the course of the time the Assamese press took off and gained a self -sufficient status. Administrative machinery appeared to use it at a later stage. Today, the Assamese press has got a status which is well recognized in India. Thus, the Indian press as well as the Assamese press provides the two flanks of a historical- professional environment of the Barak Valley press within its regional setting.

The press in the valley emerged and grew in the environment and consciousness of the Indian freedom movement among the intellectuals. Local problems were consciously brought to the notice of the administration and the masses through a good number of press publications. The valley press originated from indigenous Indian source as the journalists and intellectuals were mostly the Bengali and were inspired by the activities of press in the mainland of Bengal surrounding Kolkata and Dhaka. No doubt, the social, political and administrative climate was not much conducive for the development of press, but the nationalist zeal and cultural enthusiasm constantly inspired the intellectuals to carry on the spirit of journalism. Independence of India infused a strong bout of spirit for nation-building in the press and it started to take strides towards professionalism and expansion among the masses.

The Independence led to a flutter of the press with many more publications of newspapers and magazines in the valley. From all the three towns the publications rolled out frequently along with the circulations of the Calcutta based newspapers. Gradually, some of the locally emerging publications got established and replaced the Calcutta based newspaper in many respects but not in totality as the diversity of population and local conditions till date offer the conditions for survival of various publications - national, regional and local. Moreover, after Independence the press changed not only in the spirit and objectives of publication but also in the contents and technology. The press gradually brought into its coverage various news, themes and sections of society. But the political news and themes dominated the press. Alongwith growing print technology, professionalism and political importance the journalism has been coming under the eclipse of yellow journalism. The press in Barak Valley, particularly the newspapers, are continuing to shape and mould the destiny of the valley through information and education. They are an effective and economical medium for creating awareness and advertising image building, opinion moulding and attitudinal changes. Today, the press is of paramount significance to achieve commercial goal and social objectives. In the valley, numerous newspapers and magazines appear and re-appear, yet only a small number of these sustain. But the publication entrepreneurship itself is a symbol of the consciousness among the people of the valley.

II

The Findings

The following are the findings of the sutdy

1. At present there are six dailies and some other periodicals like weeklies, bi-weeklies, and fortnightlies. In Barak Valley the newspapers have been emerging and published in a good number and from every corner after the publication of the first newspaper 'Silchar' in 1889. But, in reality, most of the newspapers published regularly maintain only a file copy to get advertisements from the government. The rate of appearance of newspapers in the valley is almost equal to the rate of their death from the very early stage to the present. Among the newspapers of this decade, the 'Sonar Cachar', 'Jugasankha' and Samayik Prasanga are leading in the valley.

   The newspapers reflect new trends also. The newspapers have started to publish photographs to narrate a story in a better way. Advertisements also appeared in the pages of newspapers. Both, public and government advertisements are now given in the newspapers of the valley, which help the newspapers to maintain the expenditure and to earn money. Offset press is also used to publish the newspapers. Hand composing is being replaced by computer composing. The newspapers are also brought out in standard size. Using modern technology the papers are undergoing the modernization of their publication. Daily newspapers have started various sections; viz, sports, children, women and so on. Two eminent daily newspapers; namely, Sonar Cachar and Jugashankha, have very recently started to the publish magazines with their Sunday issues. Newspapers conduct debates on various current issues and receive responses from large number of the people. The daily newspapers have also built various departments of establishment; viz, advertisement, circulation and editorial. They have set up their advertisement offices in different places of India like Delhi, Mumbai, Kolkata, Guwahati and so on. Their correspondents are found in some cities in India to give coverage of national events. Recently, the two important dailies of the valley; namely, 'Sonar Cachar' and 'Jugashankha' have introduced the Internet edition of their newspapers. They have made the web pages and send the papers on line to make their reach to the millions of people all over the world.

By their standard and contents the newspapers are, by and large, found to adore the influential political figures. Even the regularly published newspapers have only a little influence over the masses as the newspapers are more guided by the ruling class or parties than the sorrows and sufferings of the common people. The number of regular magazines is very few. Small magazines publish the views of young generation, their personal problems and so on. Now-a-days, students of schools and colleges are becoming very much career-oriented and they don't feel to write or expose themselves to the public. Moreover, they don't get the impetus from the teachers which is very much essential in developing their creativity. The news magazines and commercial magazines are generally facing the lack of financial support to bring out the magazines.

2. During the history of one hundred and fifty years of journalism in Barak Valley, the printing press and publication of newspaper have made the knowledge cheaper and easier and thereby, made a powerful impact on the transition of society from medievalism to modern period. 'Silchar', a weekly newspaper, is considered to be the first newspaper in the valley. But for how many years it existed, is known through no document. At the initial stage of the press in the valley most of the publications served the purpose of both a newspaper and a magazines, and it laid emphasis on content instead of form. Moreover, in many respects the papers were managed by an individual's resources and mission. Besides a few professional journals, numerous magazines and periodicals appeared in the period have been literary in character and managed by organizations and associations.

3. Although the wheel of journalism had started moving in Barak Valley since the last part of 19th century, it played only a little role in awakening the masses against the British Raj, notwithstanding the reproduction of news of Calcutta based newspapers. Only 'Silchar' and 'Surma' in particular more or less tried to raise the voice against the British Raj through their circulation which was confined to limited number of people. So, the two newspapers influenced the masses of the valley, though Calcutta based newspapers dominated the people of this valley. These newspapers were also brought out with coverage of the events of Barak Valley. Moreover, the Sylhet based newspapers were also there and they had also influence over the valley people. As before Independence, the valley was associated with Sylhet, it was easy for the Sylhet based newspapers to hit the stand and they did it. Actually, the newspapers in the Barak Valley faced the hindrances of market capture during the British period. Besides, the lack of proper infrastructure is responsible for the poor growth of the newspapers in the valley. Several newspapers in the Barak Valley had little influence over the masses as these newspapers preferred, in their publications, the news-contents taken from Calcutta and Sylhet based newspapers to the news about local problems.

4. In the field of journalism in Barak Valley, the journalists of Barak Valley contributed a lot in the pre-and post-Independence period. The journalists of Barak Valley took active role in disseminating news from different parts of the country. By their occupation they have been lawyers, politicians, professional journalists, educators and intellectuals. The famous lawyer Upendra Shankar Dutta was the correspondent (Silchar) of 'The Statesmen' of Silchar for a long time. The veteran journalist, H. A. Barlaskar, was associated as a correspondent with the 'Dainik Satyayug' for a long time. Late Pijush Choudhury was the correspondent of ' Ananda Bazar Patrika' and ' Hindustan Sangbad. Lawyer N. C. Shayam was the editor of 'Surma' and 'Bhabishat' who contributed in the field of journalism in Barak Valley. The politician Late M. Purakayastha was a correspondent of ' The Free Press Journal' and U. N. I. Late Ravikanta Sen was the correspodent of PTI in Silchar for a long time. The veteran journalist Amit Kr. Nag was the correspondent 'Jugantar' and 'Amrit Bazar Patrika'. Atin Das also worked as a correspondent in Silchar.

   The eminent journalist Bidhu Vushan Choudhury worked as a correspondent of U. N. I for a long time. D. K. Dutta was a correspondent of 'Ananda Bazar Patrika' and 'Hindustan Standard'. R. C. Das was the correspondent of PTI and S. R. Biswas was the correspondent of 'Dainik Bashumati'. Shaktidhar Choudhury was associated with 'Amrit Bazar Patrika', 'Jugantar' and 'The Assam Tribune'. U. Roy was a correspondent of 'Danik Basuamti' and U. N. I At present Santanu Ghosh is associated with 'The Telegraph'. Mr. Jyotilal Choudhury is associated with 'The Sentinel'. Uttam Kr. Saha is working with Ananda Bazar Patrika. At Present, Mr Himashish Bhattacharjee is the correspondent of PTI in Silchar.

5. The Barak Valley is lacking a proper infrastructure for newspaper production. Due to monetary problems the newspapers often ceased their publications. Per capita income of valley people is also low, which affects the readership. The people are inclined to read newspapers regularly but still the readership is limited. Illiteracy is also a considerable factor for the obstacle in development of the press in Barak Valley. Transport and communication facilities are also limited to facilitate the newspapers to reach out in time in every corner of the valley. The Calcutta and Delhi based Bengali and English newspapers also compete with and limit the circulation of the valley-based newspapers.

In Barak Valley, the Government and the private advertisement are very less. In this remotest part of the country the private agencies are not found. Therefore, there is no question of private business advertisements while the newspaper industry generally thrives on advertisement. The condition hampers not only the development of newspapers but also causes their early death. It is a regular phenomenon of the newspapers in the valley. The newspapers of this valley are not commercially viable.

6. Though the professionalism in the newspapers had started to appear by the time of Independence, it has yet to come up in the valley in Barak Valley. The journalists have proficiency in language, but not professionalism. Generally, they donot receive proper training. The power of press has not been properly perceived by today's Barak Valley journalists. So, the professional vision is not found both in the newspapers and journalists. The journalists of the valley have to work with little remuneration. In the press organization there is a lack of motivation and incentives for their personnel. In the present scenario, the newspapers are competing with electronic media in other parts of the country, but this competition is totally absent in this region. Interestingly, the study reveals that the women's readership is increasing.

When one looks towards the other valley of Assam, i.e, Bhramhaputra Valley, one finds the rapid increasing number of newspapers. As per the RNI record, there were only four Asssamese dailies published from Guwahati in 1990s. Today, there are twelve Asssamese dailies published from Guwahati. Moreover, the newspapers are coming out with sensational news. It is quite interesting to note that the advertising revenue of the vernacular newspapers of Assam is very low. So, the question is how these newspapers survive without financial support. The question remains enigma. Till date, not a single daily has ceased its publication. The question leads to a supposed nexus of the press with some illegitimate funding agencies, e. g., insurgents, underworld or else. The question indicates a significant problem for investigations.

Besides the contextual (geographical, economic and technological) constraints, the press in the valley is constrained by its historical legacy. The press emerged in response to the national movement and then it incorporated to local issues into its nationalist fold. After the Independence it did look the issues of nation-building and development of people. But gradually the politics acquired dominance over other aspects of life and therefore the press also started paying more attention to political issues. Besides this, the press took up various economic and social issues in a politicalized way or with political motives. Hence, the politics in journalism and the journalism in politics. This situation has helped the yellow journalism rise in the valley. The journalism appears overdominated by the politics. The weakness of the journalism may be overcome only by development of real professionalism through proper training and thereby improvement of the financial conditions of the press establishments in the valley.

III

The Significance

This is a region-specific study of press in India. There are the studies of press but they are generally historical, narrative, legalistic or rhetoric. There are not many studies conducted in the historical and contemporary context of the regional society, culture and people. This is an attempt to gather historical, oral and observed data and to determine the status of press in the Barak Valley. So far, no comprehensive study of this region has been conducted to understand the origin, growth and development of press.

Therefore, the study brings in relief the point that for understanding of a country's press in a perspective, there should be conducted local and regional level studies of press in the historical and contextual settings. The findings abstracted from these studies may be integrated together to build a theoretical system to explain the nature and changes in press in the country.

Besides, the studies of press in India have mostly depended on the data collected from historical and legal-statutory documents. These studies cannot give a real picture of the press working amidst the people. Therefore, a research design that aims to collect and analyse historical, oral, documentary and observed data has to be applied for a study of press.

The present study has attempted to use such a research design and methodology. Therefore, the study has indicated here for developing a theoretical framework for studies on the press in India, which has been lacking in the studies conducted so far. The study has also pointed out a few questions related to revenues, organization, training and ethics of press. These issues may be taken up for future investigation in regional and national setting with help of the framework indicated in the present study.

BARAK VALLEY AT A GLANCE *

Particulars	Cachar	Karimganj	Hailakandi
Geographical area	3,786 Sq.Km	1509 Sq Km	1327 Sq Km
Population 2001	1442141	1003678	542978
Male Population 2001	741580	516408	280912
Female Population 2001	700561	487270	262066
Literacy rate 2001	68.42%	67.21%	59.84%
Male literacy rate 2001	76.51%	73.87%	68.47%
Female literacy rate 2001	59.85%	60.09%	50.65%
Growth rate of Population (1991-2001)	18.66%	21.35%	20.92
No. of Subdivisions	02	01	01
No. of revenue circles	06	05	04
No. of Community dev. Blocks	15	7	5
No. of Goan Panchayats	163	96	62
No. of villages	1051	940	331
No. of Mahukuma Parisads	02	01	01
No. of Govt. Rly Out post	01	01	01
No. of Municipal Broads	01	01	01

No. of Census Towns (2001 census)	07	03	03
No. of General Colleges	15	09	07
No. of Engg. Colleges	01	Nil	Nil
No. of Medical Colleges	01	Nil	Nil
Total Population of Scheduled Language	1155993	790275	432814
No. of B.T. Colleges	01	01	00
No. of law Colleges	01	01	00
No. of High Schools	146	92	39
No. of H. S Schools	28	25	09
No. of Middle Schools	410	347	260
No. of Primary &Pre Primary School	1715	1406	1129
No. of University	01	Nil	Nil
No. of Tea Gardens	57	38	24

Source : Assam Statistical Handbook 2004

INVENTORY

ORIGIN, GROWTH AND DEVELOPMENT OF THE PRESS IN THE BARAK VALLEY.

Name of the Newspaper	Year of Origin	Present Status	Periodicity Publication	Editor	Language	Place of	Remarks
1	2	3	4	5	6	7	8
SILCHAR	1889	Not Existing	Weekly	Bidhu Busan Roy	Bengali	Silchar	-
SURMA	1911	Not Existing	Weekly	B M. Bidyarnava N.C. Shyme H.A Barlaskar	Bengali	Silchar	Resumed on 1930s
THE EASTERN CHRONICLE	1914	Not Existing	Weekly	S. Singh	English	Karimganj	-
JANASAKTI	1923	Continuing	Weekly	B.B.Chakborty & present Editor Manju Gupta	Bengali	Silchar	Irregularly
BHABISHAT	1926	Not Existing	Fort-nightly	N.C. Shyme	Bengali	Silchar	-
PANCHA-JANAYA	1930	Not Existing	Weekly	S.K. Roy	Bengali	Karimganj	-

CACHAR	1932	Not Existing	Weekly	M. Choudhury	Bengali	Silchar	-
SAPTAK	1937	Not Existing	Weekly	Kushimohan Das	Bengali	Silchar	-
VIJOYNINY	1939	Not Existing	Monthly	Ms. J. Chanda	Bengali	Silchar	-
MANIPURI	1939	Not Existing	Weekly	S. Singh	Manipuri	Silchar	-
SAMABAY	1939	Not Existing	Fort-nightly	B.K. Aditya	Bengali	Karimganj	-
PANCHA-JAYA	1940	Not Existing	Weekly	H.R. Bhattacharjee	Bengali	Silchar	-
ADIKAR	1943	Not Existing	Weekly	A. Kr. Battacarjee	Bengali	Hailakandi	-
JUGASHAKTI	1945	Continuing	Weekly	B.B.Chouhury & present Editor Bijit Choudhury	Bengali	Karimjanj	-
AZAD HIND	1948	Not Existing	Weekly	M. A Laskar	Bengali	Silchar	-
MUKTI PRADIP	1948	Not Existing	Weekly	Baidanath Nath	Bengali	Silchar	-
FARIYAD	1948	Not Existing	Weekly	J. A. Barlaskar	Bengali	Silchar	-
AGNIBAN	1949	Not Existing	Weekly	Subimol Endow	Bengali	Silchar	-

1	2	3	4	5	6	7	8
CHROMIK	1950	Continuing	Weekly	M. Purkasthya & Present Editor Siva Prasad Baidya	Bengali	Silchar	-
ARUNODOI	1950	Continuing	Weekly	S.Dutta Roy & Present Editor Chandan Sengupta	Bengali	Silchar	-
PURBANCHAL	1950	Not Existing	Weekly	Subodh Ch. Dutta	Bengali	Karimjanj	-
CACHAR	1950	Not Existing	Weekly	S.S. Bhadra	Bengali	Hailakandi	Resumed on 1972 but dis-continued
CHRONICLE	1950	Not Existing	Weekly	P. Goswami	English	Silchar	-
SHIMANTIK	1950	Not Existing	Weekly	N. Bhattacharya	Bengali	Karimganj	-
AZAD	1951	Not Existing	Weekly	H.A. Barlaskar	Bengali	Silchar	-
NABAJUG	1955	Continuing	Weekly	R. ch. Biswas & Present Editor Rahul Das	Bengali	Karimjanj	-

JUGASHANKA	1959	Continuing as Daily	Weekly	Baidanath Nath & present Editor Santano Ghose	Bengali as a Daily on 19th May 1995	Silchar	Resumed
PURBASHREE	1962	Not Existing	Weekly	D. Kumar Das	Bengali	Silchar	-
DRISTIPAT	1963	Not Exiting	Weekly	Dakhi-naranjan Deb	Bengali	Karimjanj.	Also published in Dimasa language from Halflong
RUPANTAR	1964	Not Existing	Weekly	P. Paul Choudhury	Bengali	Silchar	-
ALOK	1966	Not Existing	Weekly	J.M. Barbiuya	Bengali	Silchar	-
BARAK	1966	Continuing		A. F. Osamni & present Editor Atin Das	Bengali	Silchar`	-
DHALESWARI	1966	Not Existing	Weekly	Nanigopal Dey	Bengali	Hailakandi	-
GATI	1966	Continuing	Daily	Jatin Deb Roy	Bengali	Silchar	1984 resumed as daily but earlier Weekly

1	2	3	4	5	6	7	8
PRANTIYA SAMACHAR	1968	Not Existing	Weekly	Attaur R. Khan	Bengali	Silchar	-
PURBAYAN	1969	Continuing	Weekly	S. Choudhury & Presently Nitish Bhatt	Bengali	Hailakandi	-
MATRIBHUMI	1970	Not Existing	Weekly	N.Kishore Singha & latter P. Paul Choudhury	Bengali	Silchar	Resumed on 1979 but disconti- nued
HUCHIYAR	1970	Not Existing	Weekly	M. Barlsakar	Bengali	Silchar	-
CACHAR TRIBUNE	1970	Not Existing	Weekly	Ujjal Kr Das	English	Hailakandi	-
AI TO SWADESH	1970	Conituing	Bi-weekly	Taj Uddin Barbhuiya	Bengali	Silchar	-
NABADIGANTA	1970	Not Existing	Weekly	A.M.Barbhuiya	Bengali	Silchar	-
MAHANAYAK	1971	Not Existing	Weekly	N. Choudhury	Bengali	Karimjanj	-
UMACHAL	1971	Not Existing	Fort- nightly	Imanuddin Bulbul	Bengali	Silchar	-

NABARUN	1974	Not Existing	Weekly	Suranjan Dutta	Bengali	Karimjanj	-
ANKUSH	1975	Not Existing	Fort-nightly	Atin Das	Bengali	Silchar	-
YUBABANI	1975	Not Existing	Fort-nightly	K.D.A.Majumdar	Bengali	Silchar	-
CACHAR SAMACHAR	1977	Not Existing	Weekly	B. K. Choudhury	Bengali	Silchar	-
SAMAYIK PRASANGA	1977	Continuing	Daily	T. Raja Choudhury	Bengali	Silchar	-
DALIM	1978	Not Exiting	Weekly	J R Mazumdar	Bengali	Hailakandi	-
AGNIBAN	1979	Not Exiting	Weekly	Haripada Dey	Bengali	Karimjanj.	-
DIBAKAR	1980	Continuing	Weeekly	Alaya Mazumdar	Bengali	Lala, Hailakandi	-
GARGHAR SANHATI	1980	Not Existing	Weekly	R.S. Mazumdar	Bengali	Silchar	-
MAHAKAL	1980	Not Exiting	Weekly	Jalanta Sengupta	Bengali	Hailakandi	-
CACHAR TIMES	1982	Continuing	Bi weekly	Dipon Dewanji	Bengali	Silchar	-
VARTA LIPI	1982	Continuing	Weekly	P. Bhattacharjee	Bengali	Silchar	-
ANANDAJYOTI	1983	Not Existing	Weekly	J.Goswami	English	Karimganj	-

1	2	3	4	5	6	7	8
GANASURYA	1984	Not Existing	Weekly	Chandan Ghose	Bengali	Silchar	-
NABABARTA PRASANGA	1986	Continuing	Bi-weekly	H.R. Choudury	Bengali	Karimjanj	-
KACHAR LIPIKA	1986	Continuing	Weekly	Mitu Bhattacharjee	Bengali	Silchar	-
BARAK DARPAN	1985	Continuing	Weekly	Bably Adhikary	English	Silchar	-
CHALLANGER VARTA	1985	Continuing	Weekly	B.Bhattacharya	English	Karimganj	-
MILLATER DAK	1988	Continuing	Weekly	Moulana I. Ahmed	English	Silchar	-
MITRIBANI	1989	Not Existing	Fort-nightly	S.K. Das	English	Silchar	-
JANAMAN	1992	Not Existing	Weekly	M.Hasan	Bengali	Karimganj	-
AMAR BARAK	1993	Continuing	Weekly	N.Dhar	Bengali	Silchar	-
SILCHAR TIMES	1994	Continuing	Daily	S.K.Kairy	Bengali	Silchar	-
SAPATH		Not Existing	Weekly	K. Bhattachajee	Bengali	Silchar	-

THE FORNTIER SUN		Continuing	Daily	Mridul Roy	English	Silchar	Single English Daily of Barak Valley
SENAPATI		Not Existing	Weekly	M.Haque Choudhry	Bengali	Karimjanj	-
NAYA CACHAR		Not Existing	Weekly	S.K. Purkayastha	Bengali	Silchar	-
PRANTOJYOTI		Not Existing	Daily	Jyotindra Dutta	Bengali	Silchar	The first daily of Barak Valley
DONKA		Not Existing	Weekly	K.Ch. Bhattacarjee	Bengali	Karimjanj	-
TRITHABHUMI	-	Not Existing	Weekly	Satu Roy	Bengali	Karimjanj	-
SONAR DESH	-	Continuing	Weekly	Prangopal Roy	Bengali	Silchar	-
PURBA DIGANTA	-	Not Existing	Weekly	H.Kumar Singh	Bengali	Silchar	-
ISAN KAUN	-	Continuing	Weekly	Amar Singh	Bengali	Silchar	Irregularly published
AANCHOLIK	-	Not Existing	Weekly	Sajal Kanti Biswas		Bengali	Silchar -

1	2	3	4	5	6	7	8
PRABAH	-	Not Existing	Weekly	Kafil Ahmed	Bengali	Badarpur	-
ASSAM DARPAN	-	Not Existing	Weekly	Dulal Mitra	Bengali	Silchar	-
SAMAYIK UPAHAR	-	Not Exiting	Weekly	Swapan Kr. Deb	Bengali	Silchar	-
PRANTA REKHA	-	Not Existing	Weekly	Biman Bihari Deb	Bengali	Silchar	-
KUSHIARA	-	Continuing	Weekly	R.K. Banik	Bengali	Karimganj	Irregularly published
AGAMI SHATABDI	-	Continuing	Weekly	Uma Roy	Bengali	Silchar	-
PALLIBANI	-	Continuing	Fort-nightly	J.H. Majumdar	Bengali	Silchar	-
SHIBAYAN	-	Not Existing	Weekly	N.Paulchoudhury	Bengali	Silchar	-
BARAK PRABHAHA	-	Not Existing	Weekly	D.Singha	Bengali	Silchar	-
TURJA	-	Weekly	S.K.Deb	Bengali	Silchar	-	
DHANURBAN	-	Not Existing	Weekly	K.Das	Bengali	Silchar	-

JAGO	-	Not Existing	Fortnightly	A.Das & J.Bhatt & S. Biswas	Bengali	Silchar	-
BARTAMAN	-	Not Existing	Weekly	V.Shyam	Bengali	Silchar	-
MUKTINAYAK	-	Not Existing	Weekly	A.Chakraborty	Bengali	Silchar	-
ASSAMSHIRSHA	-	Not Existing	Weekly	S.Biswas	Bengali	Silchar	-
JANAMAT	-	Not Existing	Weekly	A. Sengupta	Bengali	Hilakandi	-
SHATABHISHA	-	Not Existing	Weekly	H. Dutta	Bengali	Karimganj	-
KARIMGANJ SANBAD	-	Not Existing	Weekly	R. Roy	Bengali	Karmganj	-
DAK DIYA JAI	-	Not Existing	Fort-nightly	S.U.Badalaskar	Bengali	Badajatra-pur	-
PALLIBANI	-	Not Existing	Weekly	S.Roy	Bengali	Silchar	-
THE EASTERN GARDIAN	-	Not Existing	Weekly	S.Gosh	English	Silchar	-
NAYA DUNIYA	-	Not Existing	Weekly	J.Das	Bengali	Karimganj	-
STAR	-	Not Existing	Weekly	M.Dutta	English	Silchar	-
JAGARAN	-	Not Existing	Weekly	Bengali	Silchar	-	

1	2	3	4	5	6	7	8
SHIMANTIK	-	Not Existing	Weekly	M. Bhattacharjee	Bengali	Silchar	-
NABASHAKTI	-	Not Existing	Weekly	A.Kar	Bengali	Silchar	-
THE ESTERN FRONTIER TIMES	-	Not Existing	Weekly	K.D.Crody	English	Silchar	-
THE VOICE	-	Not Existing	Weekly	K.S. Purkaystha	English	Hailakandi	-
PRANTIK	-	Not Existing	Weekly	A.Choudhury	Bengali	Hilakandi	-
JANAKALYAN	-	Not Existing	Weekly	H.Paul	Bengali	Silchar	-
NABADHARA	-	Not Existing	Weekly	P.Purkaystha	Bengali	Hilakandi	-
SHAJAAG	-	Not Existing	Weekly	S.Choudhury	Bengali	Hilakandi	-
JAGARANI	-	Not Existing	Weekly	N.Choudhury	Bengali	Silchar	-
NAGARIK	-	Not Existing	Weekly	L.Kar	Bengali	Karimganj	-
NABAYAN	-	Not Existing	Fort-nightly	Hariprashanna Sen	Bengali	Hilakandi	-

Bibliography

Aggarwal, Vir Bala 1992 *Mass Media in Rural Development: Some Research Issues, Communicator,* December.

Agree, Waren K., 1977 *Introduction to Mass Communication,* New York: Harper and Row Publishers.

Ault Philip, H., Emery Edwin and Ahuja, B.N 1998 *Mass Communication,* New Delhi: Allied Publishers.

Apte, Mahadeb L 1978 *Mass Culture, Language, Arts, In India,* Bombay: Popular Prakashan.

Bagchi Geopab Pallab Mukhodheya 1997 *Mass Communication and Social Development, Communicator,* April-June

Baghel, D.S. 1975 *Social Control and Social Change,* Reewa: Pushparaj Prakashan.

Baruah, Sunil Pawan 1999 *Press in Assam: Origin and Development*, Guwahati: Lawer Book Stall.

Barketaki, S 1969 *Assam,* New Delhi: National Book Trust.

Basu, Jitendra 1979 *Romance of Indian Journalism,* Calcutta: Calcutta University Press.

Bashiruddin, S 1980 *Rural Press in India, AMIC:* Bangalore.

Bhagati, Radhika Mohan 2005 *Sambad Sambadpatra Aru Sambadikata*, Guwahati: Publication Board of Assam.

Bhatnagar, S, and Chib, S.S. 1987 *Rural Development in India, A strategy for Socio-economic Change,* New Delhi: Ess Publication.

Bhatnagar, Ram Ratan 1947 *The Rise and Growth of Hindi Journalism,* Allahabad: Kitab Mahal.

Bhattacharjee, Asit 1998 *Press as a Catalyst of Social and Economic change,* in Dua, M.R. (ed.), *Press as leader of society,* New Delhi.: IIMC & Press Council of India

Bhattacharjee, Bijit Kumar 2000 *Atandra O Barak Upatakaya Bangla Kayaba Charcha,* Hailakandi: Sahitya Prakashan.

Bhattacharjee, Bijit Kumar 2002 *Uttar Purva Bharater Bangla Sahitiya,* Hailakandi: Sahitya Prakashan.

Bhattacharjee, J.B. 1986 *Studies in the History of North-East India,* Shillong: Publication.

Bhattacharjee, Jatin Mohan 1942 *Srihattabashi Sampadiya Abong Srihatta O Cachar Haite Prakashito Sambad Patrika,* Syleth: Sarada Printing and Publishing Limited.

Bhattacharjee, Usharanjan 1993 *Srihatta Sahitya Parishat O Patrika,* Calcutta: Oriental Publishers.

Bhargava, M 1987 *Role of Press in the Freedom Movement,* New Delhi: Reliance Publishers.

Bhatt, C.S. 1997 *Indian Press 1955,* New Delhi: Publication Division, Ministry of Information and Broadcasting, Government of India.

Bhum, Eleanor 1963 *Reference Books in the Mass Media,* Urbana: University of Illinois.

Bialock, H.M. 1972 *Social Statistics,* Tokyo: McGraw-Hill Kogakusha Ltd.

Blackburn, Robin 1977 *Ideology in Social Science,* Fontana: Collins.

Brahmananda 1986 *Bharatiya Swatantrata Andolon Aur Uttar Pradesh Ki Hindi Patrika,* New Delhi: Vani Prakashan.

Bryson, Lyman 1948 *The Communication of Ideas,* New York: Harper.

Carpenter, Edmund S. and Marshall McLuhan 1960 *Explorations in Communication,* Boston: Beacon Press.

Carter, Roy F. Jr. 1958 *Newspaper, Gatekeepers and the Sources of News, Public Opinion Quarterly* 22: Summer.

Casty, Alan 1969 *Mass Media and Mass Man,* New York: Holt Rinehart and Winston.

Chakraborty, A 1989 *History of Education in Assam,* Delhi: Mittal Publishers Pvt. Ltd

Chatterjee, S 2000 *Socio-Economic History of South Assam,* Jaipur: P.W. Publishers.

Choudhury, Loho Biplap 1998 *NE Press fails to rise to occasion, Communicator:* April-June.

Chauhan, Swasti and Chandra Nar 1985 *Journalism Today – Principles, Practices and Challenges,* New Delhi: Kanishka Publishers & Distributors .

Choudhury Dutta, Mondira 2002 *Impact of Modernization on the Traditional Institute of the Barmans of the Barak Valley: 1947-1990,* PhD Thesis, Silchar: Assam University.

Clarke, Peter and F. Gerald Kline 1974 *Media effects reconsidered: some new strategies for communication research, Communication Research.*

Cosh, M John 1986 *Topography of Assam,* Delhi: Logos Press

Curran, Gurevitch and Woollacott Edward Arnold 1977 *Mass Communication and Society,* Open University Press.

Das, Atin 2002 *Satabdir Taithya Punji, Barak Upatakaya Banga Sahitya Sambelan,* Silchar: Prasongik Printers and Publication.

Das, Kaliprasana 1964 *Sambadpatra Sebay Srihatter Sthan,* Shillong.

Dexter, Lewis A, and White, David Manning 1964 *People Society and Mass Communications,* New York: The Free Press.

Dhama, O.P. and O.P. Bhatnagar 1980 *Education and Communication Development,* New Delhi: Oxford.

Dhar Nath Som 1998 *A Mirror of the Society* in Dua, M. R. (ed), *Press as Leader of Society,* Hyderabad: University of Hyderabad.

Dube, S.C. 1980 *Problems of Nation-building: Not by Economic Development Alone, The Times of India,* July.

Dutta, P.N. 1962 *Glimpses into the History of Assam*, Guwahati.
Dua, H.K. 1998 *Role of Press as Ombudsman of Society*, in Dua, M. R. (ed) *Press as Leader of Society*, New Delhi: IIMC and Press Council of India.

Ghosh, Subir 1991 *Mass Media Today,* Calcutta: Profile Publisher.

Goode and Hatt 1952 *Methods in Social Research,* Tokyo: McGraw-Hill Kogakusha Ltd.

Gujral, U.K. 1973 *Mass Communication and Development, Mainstream*, 12, Annual.

Hardikar, A.R. 1996 *Aim and Objective of Media in Present Stuation Communicator,* July-Sept.

Hartman, Paul 1989 *The Mass Media and Village Life: An Indian Study,* New Delhi: Sage Publication.

Joseph, Ammu 1997 *Press in India-Priorities, Mainstream*: October 4.

Joseph, M.K 1996 *Modern Media and Communication, Mass Media and Challenge of Change,* New Delhi: Anmol Publication Pvt. Ltd.

Joshi, P.C. 1985 *Communication and Nation-Building-Perspectives and Policy,* New Delhi: Publication Division.

Kain, R.L. 1998 *Press and its Accountabilityto the Society,* in Dua, M.R. (ed) *Press as Leader of Society,* IIMC and Press Council of India, New Delhi.

Kalra, C.S. 1998 *Press as a Tribune to the Society,* in Dua, M.R. (ed) *Press as Leader of Society,* New Delhi: IIMC and Press Council of India.

Kumar, J. Keval 1981 *Mass Communication in India*, Mumbai: Jaico Publishing House.

Kumar, Monohar Manoj 1994 *Regional Language Media: Problems and Prospects,*

Communicator, April-June.

Kuppuswamy, B 1976 *Communication and Social Development in India,* Bombay: Sterling Publication.

Kuppuswamy, B 1977 *Social Change in India*, New Delhi: Vikas Publishing House

Lerner, D. and Wilbur Schramm 1969 *Communication and Change in the Developing Countries,* Honolulu: East-West Center Press.

Mahiudin, Siru 1992 *Sylether Satabarsher Sambad Patra,* Syleth: Akkhar Computer.

Mankekar, R.D 1973 *The Press under Pressure,* New Delhi: Indian Book Company.

Malhan, P.N. 1986 *National Media Policy, Vidura:* February.

Malhan, P.N. 1995 *For whom the media*? in A.K. Banerjee (ed.), *Communication and Development, UGC Special Assistance Programme,* Vanarasi: *Deptt, of Journalism and Communication,* Banaras Hindu University.

Mcouli, Denis 1969 *Towards a Sociology of Mass Communication,* London.: Collier-Macmillan Limited.

Mehta, D.S. 1979 *Mass Communication and Journalism in India,* New Delhi: Allied Publishers.

Mehra, S.R. 1992 *Democratization and Development in Communication and Development: Issues and Perspectives,* Jaipur: Rawat Publications.

Mathur, K.V. 1996 *Communication for Development and Social Change,* New Delhi: Allied Publishers.

Mazumdar, A 1996 *Statistical People of Barak Valley and An Agenda For Research on Valley's Economy*, North-Eastern Centre For Advanced Studies, Silchar:

Mohanty, B.B. 1990 *Media and National Integration, Communicator,* September.

Mohapatra, Chintamoni 1984 *The Development Coverage of Two Typical Newspapers, Vidura:* December.

Moitra, Mohir 1969 *A History of Indian Journalism,* National Book Agency Pvt. Ltd.

Mudgal, Rahul 1998 *Contemporary Issues in Journalism*, New Delhi: Sareep and Sons.

Mulgaokar, M.S. 1984 *The Press in India,* Bombay: Popular Prakashan.

Murthy, Krishna Nadig 1966 *Indian Journalism,* Mysore *'Prasaranga'*: University of Mysore.

Murthy, D.V.R. 1999 *Uses and Limits of Content Analysis in Communicator:* April-June

Nag, Amit Kumar 2000 *Assamer Batri Kakat Abcanir Dersa Barchariya Itihass*, Guwahati: Tribune Press.

Nath, R.M. 1981 *Antiquities of Cachar*, Silchar.

Natrajan, S, 1962 *History of Press in India,* Bombay: Popular Prakashan.

Nayar, Kuldeep 1977 *The Judgment,* New Delhi: Vikas Publishing House.

Neogi, Gautam 1977 *Role of Press in India's Struggle for Independence*: *Historical Judgment,* Indian Journalists Association, Platinum Jubilee Commemoration Volume.

Padhya, S.K 1991 *Battle of Freedom of the Press in India,* New Delhi: Academic Foundation.

Padhya, S.K and Sahu, N.R. 1997 *The Press In India - Perspective in Development and Relevance,* New Delhi: Kanishka Publishers and Distributors.

Pandey, G.P 1999 *Press and Social Change,* Delhi: Manak Publication Pvt. Ltd.

Panigrahy, Divakar 1993 *Media Management in India,* Delhi: Kanishka Publishing House.

Parthasarathy, Rangaswami 1989 *Journalism in India - From the Earliest Time to the Present Day,* New Delhi: Sterling Publishers Pvt. Ltd.

Pool, Ithiel de Sola 1959 *Trends in Content Analysis,* Urbana: University of Illinois Press.

Raghavan, S.N.G 1994 *The Press in New History,* New Delhi: Gyan Publishing House.

Rao, Kalpana Tellu 1994 *Social Responsibility of Press In 21st Century, Communicator,* April-June.

Ratan T 1990 *Encyclopedia of North-East India,* Delhi: Kalpaz Publication.

Rau Chalapathi, M 1968 *The Press in India,* New Delhi: Allied Publishers Pvt Ltd.

Rau Chalapathi, M 1980 *200 Years of Indian Press, Vidura:* February.

Sankar, SCR 1984 *The Press in India,* New Delhi: S Chand and Co.

Satyanarayna Pattanaik and Daljit Singh Bedi 1997 *Language Press in India, Communicator,* Oct-Dec.

Selltiz, Claire *et al.* 1951 *Research Methods in Social Relations,* New York New Fetter Lane E.C. 4, Methuen and Co. Ltd.

Seshaiah S. and V.S. Parthasarathy, *In India,* Bombay: Allied Publishers Pvt. Ltd.

Shrivastava, K.M. 1972 *Media Issues,* New Delhi: Sterling Publication.

Smith, Anthony 1979 *The Newspaper – An International History,* London: Thames and Hudson.

Srinivas, M.N., 1977 *Dimensions of Social change.*

Tucker, Nicholas 1967 *Understanding the Mass Media,* Cambridge: Cambridge University Press.

Veeraraghavan, J. 1998 *Accountability of the Press to Society* in Dua, M.R. (ed) *Press as Leader of Society,* New Delhi: IIMC and Press Council of India.

Index

N

O

P

Q

R

S